pleasers

Also by Dr. Kevin Leman

The Birth Order Book
Making Children Mind without Losing Yours
Sex Begins in the Kitchen
The Perfect Match
Be Your Own Shrink

pleasers

*why women don't have to
make everyone happy to be happy*

Dr. Kevin Leman

Revell

Grand Rapids, Michigan

© 1987, 2006 by Dr. Kevin Leman

Published by Fleming H. Revell
a division of Baker Publishing Group
P.O. Box 6287, Grand Rapids, MI 49516-6287
www.revellbooks.com

Second printing, June 2006

New paperback edition published 2006

Previously published in 1988 under the title *Women Who Try Too Hard: Breaking the Pleaser Habits*

Printed in the United States of America

The Library of Congress Cataloging-in-Publication Data
Leman, Kevin.
    Pleasers : why women don't have to make everyone happy to be happy /
Kevin Leman.
        p. cm.
    Previously published in 1988 under the title Women who try too hard :
breaking the pleaser habits"—T.p. verso.
    Includes bibliographical references (p.   ).
    ISBN 10: 0-8007-3125-5 (pbk.)
    ISBN 978-0-8007-3125-0 (pbk.)
        1. Women—Psychology. 2. Self-esteem in women. 3. Dominance
(Psychology) 4. Assertiveness in women. I. Title.
HQ1206.L426 2006
155.6′33—dc22   2005037894

To Hannah Elizabeth Leman
Born June 20, 1987

Hannah Elizabeth

A child's warm and tender skin
Soft and smooth, without a flaw.

The small body hasn't experienced life yet—
Just being born into it—
But this is God's law.

The innocence of a child,
something we should all have—
something we should strive to be.

An innocent child, fresh in God's sight,
As she ventures out to experience life.

Holly Leman, age 14

Contents

Contents

Introduction

Do you know this woman?

Her motto in life is peace at any price. This is a woman who bites off far more than she can chew. She's responsible for other people's failures and negligence. She should have been a bail bondswoman because she's great at bailing people out of their messes.

You'd like her because she's a very nice person. Everyone else likes her too. But she wants the oceans of life smooth around her. She avoids conflict. She laughs at a joke she doesn't understand. She appears unaffected when she is offended. She's responsible for everything. If it rains at the family reunion, it's her fault because she picked the location.

She's most likely the firstborn daughter or the middle daughter. People know her soft spots. They know how to push her buttons. Many days she runs on a tankful of guilt that she can live on for a week at a time. Driven by the guilt she carries through life, she doesn't know how to say no.

Again, I ask you, do you know this person? She's the Pleaser. And in the pages that follow, *Pleasers* will teach this woman how to develop "know" power. What does that mean? Well, there's something wonderful about having a pleasing personality, and there's certainly nothing wrong with pleasing other people. Let's face it—the world would be a lot nicer place to live in if we had more people who were bent on pleasing others. But at what expense to the Pleaser and the ones she tries to satisfy?

Maybe you know this woman. Or, maybe you *are* this woman. *Pleasers* is a book written specifically for you, and for those who want to help you. Just as important, this book will help you become what I call a Positive Pleaser.

Then you can kiss the old days good-bye ... the days when you used to say yes but you really meant no.

PART 1

Portrait of the Pleaser

What is she like, this woman who wants to please? Is she motivated by fear or does she have a Florence Nightingale complex? Is it bad to be a pleaser? Does pleasing inevitably lead to being a doormat and thus a slave to a controller? Are there different kinds of pleasers? How did you get to be a pleaser? Is it inherited, like blue eyes, or did you learn it? In the first three chapters you will learn the answers to these questions, as well as

- what is the life-style of the typical pleaser?
- where do you fit on the Pyramid of Pleasers?
- why *no* is the hardest word a pleaser ever has to say
- the key characteristics of all pleasers
- how pleasers are trained from childhood to be "good little girls"
- how the "love bank" affects your relationships
- what kind of pleaser are you? This quiz will tell
- why the little girl you once were is still with you
- why your relationship to Daddy was absolutely crucial
- why you can't change "your grain" but you *can* change
- which birth order has the most pleasers
- why the youngest members of the family are the least likely to be pleasers

What Kind of Pleaser Are You?

"She always tries to make everyone happy."

She seems quite confident on the surface, but behind the "I'm working at it" smile is a woman who is a bit down. She doesn't feel as if she measures up to what life is throwing at her, and she's in my office to figure out why.

Her story pours out. She's "successful" as wife, mother, and working woman. She is busy, oh, so busy. Her schedule rivals the man who rides around in *Air Force One*. It seems her kids are involved in every activity and sport, and therefore so is she.

Her husband? Well, he's busy too, even busier than she is. He works long hours, staggers in anywhere from 7:30 to

9:45 p.m., sometimes too tired to eat, always ready to collapse on the couch and watch TV. She doesn't say anything, of course, because when she does he can get quite angry. *He's doing it all for me and the girls*, she tells herself.

This woman seems to have it all, so "Why," she asks, "am I so depressed? Why don't my kids listen to me? Why can't I say no? I even buy things from machines that call with a recorded sales pitch. Why does everyone take advantage of me? I try so hard to please. Why is everybody on my back?"

"Tell me more," I reply, usually knowing what she will say.

And the story continues to come out. She isn't as confident as her perfectly tailored suit and perfectly done face, nails, and hair suggest. She is achieving at work but doesn't feel that good about it.

"I second-guess myself," she says ruefully. "I doubt my ability even when I succeed and my boss praises me for it. I feel I should have done it better. I rethink things until I find fault with myself."

After work her balancing act continues. She rushes over to her mother's house, where her two daughters always go after school. And she gets it there with both barrels.

Her mother always worries about her health. She's working too hard. She needs more rest. How can she care for a family and work, too?

Her two daughters aren't as concerned about her rest. In fact, they want her to run a little faster. Why is she late again? What's for dinner? Can they watch TV until nine o'clock? Are they going to the zoo Saturday? Did she get the material to make the costumes for their party?

"Sometimes I just feel overwhelmed," she admits. "I don't think I can do it. Maybe my mother is right. I guess

14

I just don't have what it takes to make a good marriage today. My friends aren't doing much better. It seems as if everybody is getting divorced."

"When you were a little girl, what was it like growing up?" I ask, and she remembers having to stand on her own two feet after her dad left when she was ten.

"Mom drove him out," she recalls. "He loved me, I know he did, but he couldn't take the hassle. And when he started drinking, that was it. Mom said he had to get out and he did. I saw him only a few times after that. He was going to come to my high school graduation but something happened. . . ."

As she talks, the pattern continues. She always got good grades, always came home before curfew. She tried to be a help to her mother, who never remarried, but whatever she did, it wasn't quite good enough.

"Mom was always second-guessing me on what I wore and how I looked. She let me know in one way or another that I really wasn't adequate. All I could hope for was to snag a man, and then I could never be sure he'd hang around."

Dutifully she tried to learn all the tricks of the trade—how to be attractive, sexy, available. That was the only way she could hope to be loved. And now she had come to see me because the balancing act was getting more and more difficult. She was feeling less secure and less confident all the time. And she was beginning to suspect that her husband's frequent need to work overtime didn't always involve his accounts.

Pleasers Fall into Many Categories

The woman I have described is a composite of clients I see weekly. She represents a wide variety of the species I call "the pleasers."

They can be single, married, divorced, thinking of re-marriage, or recently remarried and in "the same bad scene again." Some have sworn off men for good and are marinating in their own bitterness, wondering if they can ever be happy.

Whatever their situation at the moment, all these women want to know why their sincere attempts to please haven't really pleased anyone, particularly themselves. Their complaints are familiar:

"Why is everyone always on my case? I try so hard to please and all I get is guff—from the kids, from the dog, from the checker at the supermarket. And oh, yes, from Ol' Harry, when he remembers to come home from work."

"Why can't I say no? I give in to my kids. I say yes, I'll collect for charity, even though I've done it for the last five years and I know there are at least three women on the block who spend most of the day having coffee and watching soaps. I'm always the one who will head the P.T.A. or church committee. I'm always the one who buys three kinds of Girl Scout cookies or the candy I don't want so somebody's high school band can go to Hawaii."

"I love him too much." This is a favorite line of the woman I call "Martha Luther" because her goal in life is to reform her man: "I knew Jim wasn't a real good catch. He drank, he didn't have steady work, and he liked to flirt—still does. But I saw something in him and I wanted to bring that out. Right now he's tearing me up inside but I know that someday he'll change. I'll just have to try harder. . . ."

"He's sleeping with another one . . . and after all I've done. I put him through school, I've raised four kids with little or no help, I keep his dinner warm at night and serve his coffee hot in the morning before he dashes off to concentrate

on his career. Well, he's concentrated, all right—on Irene, Alice, Barbara, and now it's Gerri."

"*I have to walk on eggs* and so do the kids. He flies off the handle without warning. He yells and screams, calls us horrible names. He's not always like that—he can be charming and even tender, but when the pressure is on at work, I know it gets to him. I suppose I get to him—I'm so lucky to have him but I may lose him. . . ."

At the absolute bottom of the barrel is the pleaser who is trapped in a marriage with a misogynist—a woman hater. He may abuse her physically but is more likely to wield verbal attacks and put-downs that are almost beyond description. Does his pleasing mate take offense at the obscene names he calls her? No, she simply apologizes for being a "sloppy slut" or a "selfish witch" who thinks only of herself.

Pleasers Have Certain Characteristics

As the above vignettes reveal, the problems of pleasers vary, but there are common threads in their backgrounds. Following are some of the major characteristics of the pleaser personality:

1. *These women learned to be pleasers when they were little girls.* Pleasers are often perfectionists who are heavily influenced by parental pressure. That pressure might be active and critical ("Why can't you ever do anything right?"), or it can be passive and subtly controlling ("That's okay, honey, I'll do it over. You'll learn someday").
2. *Pleasers often come from unhappy homes in which their fathers gave them very little attention, support, or love.*

17

Often Dad left while they were still young. They never learned how to relate to a male on a positive, healthy basis, and their marriages wind up disasters. In a vast majority of cases, the relationship of Daddy to his daughter is absolutely crucial. This is a point I will make again and again throughout this book.

3. *Pleasers are willing to settle for small favors.* They don't really want much out of life. They get frustrated, angry, and depressed by the way they are treated, but they put up with it, thinking it could be worse. They aren't in the mess the wife of the alcoholic down the block has to contend with. And at least their lives have a familiar "comfortable" pattern. Besides, they really don't deserve any more than what they have, do they?

4. *And that brings us to perhaps the key characteristic in almost all pleasers: low self-esteem.* Many pleasers, especially those who are in negative situations to one degree or another, seldom feel they are worth a great deal, that they are really loved, appreciated, and valued for themselves. They believe they have to earn their value and their worth, and that's why they always try to please.

   Another reflection of pleasers' low self-esteem is a feeling of always being responsible. They are always apologizing. Pleasers know "it's their fault." If only they had done it different, if only they'd said the right thing instead of the wrong thing, then perhaps everyone could have been happy.

5. *A strong characteristic of pleasers is trying to keep everyone happy.* They carefully navigate the oceans of life and make everything smooth for all on board. Peace at any price is often their motto, and they pay dearly.

6. *Pleasers usually feel inferior to men, or at least have a strong need to be "good girls" so men will approve of them.* As authors William Fezler and Eleanor Field point out in *The Good Girl Syndrome*, many women have been brought up in an atmosphere that makes them feel unworthy or at least slightly inferior *"simply because they are women!"* (italics mine).[1]

The "good girl" works hard at being obedient to authority figures, especially men. She obeys "because inherent in the Good Girl Syndrome is the belief that most people are better than you. This creates a vicious circle of frustration in which you feel unworthy because so many others are better, and you believe others are better because you feel unworthy."[2]

My term for those male authority figures is *controller*. In my practice I counsel many pleasers who have married controllers of one kind or another.

Controllers Come in Different Packages

We've already talked about the controller who is a misogynist—a woman hater who doesn't control a woman as much as he dominates her with a constant barrage of anger, abuse, and temper tantrums. Ironically, he will often repent of his outbursts, beg forgiveness, and pledge his undying love. His pleasing wife is not really fooled, but she tries to tell herself, "Maybe deep down he means it. Maybe he can change. . . ."

Other pleasers have husbands who might better fit the category of "dependent loser." Dependent losers control their wives through pity and desire to help them. Dependent losers wind up married to "Martha Luthers" who are sure they can reform their husbands and bring out that wonderful vein of gold they know is in there somewhere.

Women married to misogynists and losers make classic case studies for books such as *Women Who Love Too Much* (Robin Norwood) and *Men Who Hate Women and the Women Who Love Them* (Susan Forward and Joan Torres).[3] Women who love too much are usually in pain, as most of their living moments are spent talking about "him." They excuse his bad temper, indifference, and put-downs as hangovers from his unhappy childhood. They try to become his therapist. They read self-help books and underline key passages for him to read.

Other women are married to controllers who abuse them in more subtle ways. A key weapon used by many husbands is control of money. They are stingy at best and miserly at worst. Sometimes this comes out in bizarre ways. I recall one wife telling me her husband would beat on the walls of the bathroom when she or her daughters used too much water while taking showers.

I see four kinds of pleasers interacting with a controller's world. We'll work our way up from the woman in real pain and desperate trouble to the pleaser who is mildly aware that she gives more than she receives but puts up with it because "that's the way things are."

Supersuffering Pleaser

You suspect (or are quite sure) your husband is a misogynist—a woman hater—who controls you with his anger, abuse, put-downs, and neglect. He rarely uses physical weapons, but his verbal attacks are caustic, even vicious. You do everything you can to pacify him, make him happy, please him, but it isn't working. The more you apologize, capitulate, and beg his forgiveness, the more he labels you selfish, uncaring, and stupid. He's a master at humiliating you, especially in front of your friends and loved ones. This kind of relationship is totally negative. The situation is desperate and you need professional help.

Depressed Pleaser

You are married to a man who controls you with his weaknesses. You are a born care giver at heart and are trying to reproduce in your own family the kind of love and caring you never had at home as a child. You are "Martha Luther" trying to reform "Bill Bailey."

In your own way, you are a controller of sorts. You control indirectly, doing all you can to please as you vicariously try to experience the love and stability you never knew as a child. You would not be interested in a healthy, normal man who treated you with love and respect. He would be boring.

Instead, you prefer the "excitement" of someone who is distant, hard to reach, someone you can never quite be sure of. So you work overtime at putting far more than 50 percent of the effort into the relationship. You aren't finding this much fun. You are anxious, worried, unhappy. This isn't working but you are obsessed, almost addicted, to this man. You may be able to tolerate it for a while longer, but long range, things don't look too good. If you don't get help soon, something is going to give, because you have given just about all you have.

The pleaser/controller situations discussed above are what therapists call "pathogenic," or in simpler terms, sick. These descriptions might not fit your situation at all. You aren't in that kind of boat, but while your boat isn't sink-ing, it does have some leaks. Maybe you fit in one of the following categories:

Played-Out (Exhausted) Pleaser

"Played out" describes you quite well. Sometimes you're physically exhausted; at other times you have mentally had it. The stress of life gets to you, often between 5:00 and 7:00 p.m., which I call the "piranha hour," when everybody seems to want "a piece of Mom's flesh."

You would like to gain a little more respect from your immediate family as well as key acquaintances. You are put upon by your kids, your husband, salespersons, fellow workers, the P.T.A., your church, and so on. Everybody knows you can't say no and wouldn't dare speak up for yourself even if you wanted to. You would like to know how to stand up to the world, but you're afraid you would offend people and be labeled aggressive, a witch, or worse. You are angry and uptight inside, but you maintain a happy face for the world most of the time.

Mildly Discouraged Pleaser

Perhaps you are a pleaser who is "getting along okay," but you still feel mild anxiety. You realize you are in the ranks of those who aren't always treated fairly, and you are becoming a bit weary of it all. Life isn't as hectic for you as it is for the Played-Out Pleaser, but you'd like to make some changes. You are interested in making some strides in your own personal growth and maturity, and you want a better life for yourself and your family. You'd like to change things, not only for your own benefit but for theirs as well.

You really like being a nurturer and care giver, but you wish you could be a more confident, positive pleaser, really sure of who you are and what your role is in today's "liberated" culture.

Positive Pleaser

Positive Pleasers are nicely navigating what I call the "balance beam of life." They like who they are; they like nurturing and care giving. They have achieved a good balance between pleasing people and having people treat them with respect and pleasing behavior in return. The Positive Pleaser can be:

- assertive without being abrasive
- confident without being cocky
- self-nurturing without being selfish

I've counseled many women who thought they were Positive Pleasers, but eventually they discovered differently. A key to being a Positive Pleaser is to put your priorities in the right order. The following is the story of one woman who thought she was making all the right moves. She wound up not only discouraged and exhausted but in real pain as well.

Nadine Went out of Her Way Until . . .

Nadine, a pert, attractive, forty-three-year-old brunette fighting a few extra pounds, was a classic example of a woman who came from the old school that said a woman's place is in the home, but a man's home is his castle. She stayed in that castle for twenty-one years of her twenty-two-year marriage. The final year she moved in with her daughter during a separation prior to her divorce.

She is like many pleasers who wind up in my office because she grew up thinking, *As soon as I get out of high school, my real task in life is to find a man. A college degree is okay, but what's really important is to have a man.*

She found one. Richard seemed to fit the mold perfectly. He wanted her to stay home and "raise the children."

And Nadine did a fine job of that. She raised four children, and typical of many moms I see in my office, she made her children her Number One priority and relegated her husband to Number Two.

Things started off fairly well. Richard and Nadine seemed to get along and even communicate quite well, but as Nadine had children and started spending more and more time and attention on them, Richard found that his business was beginning to make more demands on his time.

Soon Richard had much less energy at the end of the day to devote to Nadine and the kids. Of course, Nadine was a supermom. She was first to volunteer for the school fair or the fund-raising jog-a-thon. At church, Nadine could always be counted on to teach Sunday school.

Inevitably, Richard and Nadine grew apart. There was little communication between them, yet in the community Nadine was looked up to by other women who wished they could have "as happy a family" as she did. They saw her as the woman who had everything. Nadine saw herself this way also, until she learned about Richard's affairs, which had started during the sixth year of their marriage.

"As usual, I was the last to know," she told me. "I didn't suspect anything until he got so blatant about it."

When Nadine did make the discovery, by inadvertently picking up an extension telephone while Richard was calling one of his "new friends," she was devastated. All those years she thought she had been doing the "right things."

She had done her duty. She had been responsible—and very trusting. If Richard hadn't reached the point where he didn't care about being discreet, she could have gone on indefinitely thinking her marriage was okay.

All four of the children were grown and gone by the time Nadine discovered Richard's unfaithfulness. The shock was too much and with her nest empty, Nadine didn't see anything left to save. So, she left also. By the time she came to see me, she was working as a minimum-wage clerk in a variety-goods store. She had not remarried and neither had Richard.

Nadine's dimpled face and big blue eyes had taken on the hard look that comes from being hurt and then turning bitter. Her story poured out. Life had been totally unfair. She had played the game by what she believed were the right rules. She had done what everybody told her to do, and what had it gotten her?

Nadine Pleased Everyone but Richard

When I started probing into Nadine's priorities, she took offense at first. She particularly didn't like the suggestion that it was wrong to make children Number One. But after a few sessions she began to see that if she had it to do over, she would have made more time for her husband. She was a pleaser who actually spent too much time pleasing everyone but the man she married.

She admitted that she often treated Richard like one of the children. I didn't get to talk to Richard, but my guess is that if he had come in he would have said, "I was treated like something *less* than one of the children." As Nadine and I talked, the following facts came out:

(1) They never had sex unless Nadine was sure the children were absent from the house or fast asleep; (2) vacations ended up wherever the kids wanted to go; (3) Nadine often overruled Richard in front of the children, emasculating him without realizing it; (4) she "went along" with sex but never initiated anything or ever told Richard she was pleased sexually; (5) sex was never spontaneous—Richard had to be patient and wait, "like a good little boy."

I see breakups like Nadine and Richard's all the time, and I call them tragic because they are so unnecessary. These people started out deeply in love. They had a good relationship but they didn't take care of it. Nadine, an avowed pleaser, spent too much time on the wrong things. You may think I overstate myself by suggesting that her children were the wrong things to spend time on, but I don't think so. When she put them first and Richard a distant second, and often third or fourth behind all of her other activities, there was only one way for things to go.

Nadine let her priorities get completely out of line, and she paid the price. Richard, of course, has to shoulder some of the blame. His priorities got fouled up as well when he started receiving less and less attention from Nadine. So he turned to his business, and then to other women, whom he usually met through his job responsibilities.

I have found no better way to describe what happened to the marriage of Richard and Nadine than the "love bank" analogy used by Dr. Willard Harley in his helpful book *His Needs, Her Needs: Building an Affair-Proof Marriage*. According to Dr. Harley, the "love bank" is that mental/emotional recorder deep within all of us which registers positive and negative experiences on a twenty-four-hour-a-day basis.

Dr. Harley's figurative love bank works on a principle of "deposits" and "withdrawals" of a certain amount of "love units," depending on the kind of encounter you have with the other person. He admits that his system is not supposed to represent actual scientific measurements; it is simply a way of looking at relationships. The love bank works like this:

Deposits	Withdrawals
+1 Comfortable encounter	-1 Uncomfortable encounter
+2 Feel good encounter	-2 Feel bad encounter
+3 Feel very good encounter	-3 Feel very bad encounter
+4 Super terrific encounter	-4 Terrible, horrendous encounter

Your love bank contains many different accounts, in fact, one for every person you know. Your family, friends, and acquaintances make deposits or withdrawals in your love bank every time they interact with you. As you can see, pleasant interactions result in deposits and unpleasant ones in withdrawals.

Why Nadine's Love Bank Account Became Depleted

Let's apply the love bank analogy to the marriage of Richard and Nadine. As far as Nadine was concerned, there weren't a lot of withdrawals out of Richard's account in her love bank. In other words, she was quite content with the situation. She put her energies and priorities into her children and treated Richard as she thought he should be treated. Richard went along with it without complaint. In short, he didn't make any trouble that could be interpreted as an uncomfortable or feel-bad encounter. And so Nadine went blithely along, thinking everything in the marriage was fine.

Where the trouble lay was with Nadine's account in *Richard's* love bank. After their early years of marriage, that account started to empty in a hurry. Withdrawals were made almost daily because of the way Nadine treated Richard with regard to sex and handling the children, to name just two areas where counseling revealed some problems. According to Dr. Harley's love bank system, I am sure that vacations were at least a minus three for Richard every time they happened.

Because his needs weren't being met, Richard turned elsewhere. He met women with whom he struck up relationships and, according to the love bank system, immediately opened new accounts with them as well as having them open new accounts with him. When one of Richard's relationships with a new woman reached a certain level—when she had enough deposits in his love bank—an affair would happen.

Why didn't Richard say something, you may ask. From what Nadine told me, he tried to send her some signals, but she wasn't listening. That's about as far as most men go, particularly men who marry pleasers. They let the wife take most of the responsibility for many areas, including communication. When Nadine stopped trying to communicate because she was busy with other things, Richard drifted into affairs that helped him meet his needs.

One statistic that is on a sharp rise is the number of couples who are getting divorced after twenty or more years of marriage. I believe a key reason for these divorces is that wives, primarily, and husbands as well, put their priorities in the wrong places—on the children, the house, their careers, and so on. *They put their priorities everywhere but on each other.* And the marriage slowly deteriorates. It often looks quite good on the outside, but eventually dry rot takes its toll and things crumble.

What Kind of Pleaser Are You?

As you can see, there are many ways to be a pleaser and many ways to wind up feeling not very pleased with your life. I often go out on a limb when I speak at seminars, workshops, and on talk shows and say that "most women are pleasers." It's our culture; it's the way women are brought up, the way they are trained. "Pleaser" is the role they believe they should play, even though they may be trumpeting women's rights, liberation, equal pay, and all the rest of the things that are so much a part of the scene today.

Where do you fit in the "hierarchy of pleasers?" The following quiz can give you some clues.

Score the 20 questions below as follows:

1	"That's me to a T."
2	"That's me, more or less."
3	"Not really me, but some similarities."
4	"That's not really me."
5	"Not me at all!"

_____ 1. I feel insecure and not very confident much of the time.

2. I feel I have to "walk on eggs" to keep everyone from getting
_____ angry.

_____ 3. My father was distant or unloving most of the time.

_____ 4. When I'm at the grocery store and shorted a penny or two on change, I don't ask for it.

_____ 5. I feel overpowered by my husband, boyfriend, or fiancé.

_____ 6. I feel I really can't do most things right.

_____ 7. I'm always saying, "I should have, I ought to. . . ."

_____ 8. My husband and children know how to make me feel guilty.

_____ 9. I feel like hiding, running away, not dealing with things.

_____ 10. I don't like confrontations. They're just too unpleasant.

_____ 11. I often fake it and tell others I like what they're doing or saying when I really don't.

_____ 12. If I try on six or seven pairs of shoes at the store, I feel I'm obligated to buy at least one pair.

_____ 13. I often feel as if I'm not really running my own life.

_____ 14. I don't get many "strokes" from those I love.

_____ 15. I am easily talked into choices that please other people more than they please me.

_____ 16. When I take the initiative or stand up for my rights, I feel apprehensive or embarrassed.

_____ 17. If I am ignored, insulted, or given poor service in a store or restaurant, I let it go because it isn't worth the hassle to complain.

_____ 18. I feel I have few choices or options to improve my life.

_____ 19. I don't get much respect from my mate.

_____ 20. Taking on new tasks makes me feel afraid and apprehensive.

SCORING:

25 or below You are a SUPERSUFFERING PLEASER. You are definitely in the hands of a controller or possibly a misogynist who is constantly criticizing and abusing you verbally and, on occasion, physically. You need help, probably from an outside source such as a pastor/counselor or psychiatrist/psychologist.

25-50 You are a DEPRESSED PLEASER. You have a knack for finding the losers or the losing situations in life. You are probably tied to a "megaloser" who keeps you involved with him because "he needs you." Or perhaps you are being victimized by a husband who is a womanizer, wanderer, or deadbeat who can't keep a job. You are hanging on by your fingernails but starting to slip.

50-75 You are a PLAYED-OUT PLEASER. You are making a go of life, but you often feel exhausted, put down, under the gun—as if someone's always wanting a piece of your flesh. You don't get enough respect, you wish you could stand up for your rights, but you really don't know how.

75-90 You are a MILDLY DISCOURAGED PLEASER. Life isn't all that bad. You have good times to offset the bad, but you know things could be much, much better.

91 and above You are in the POSITIVE PLEASER ranks. You like to please but have enough assertiveness and self-esteem to find fulfillment, satisfaction, and enjoyment. Your family gives you the love and support you need, and your pleasing efforts are an even exchange for that love and support.

DR. LEMAN'S PYRAMID OF PLEASERS

Positive Pleaser Good balance between pleasing nature and receiving the respect, support, and love she wants and needs.

Mildly Discouraged Pleaser Pluses usually outweigh the minuses, but she knows life could be a great deal better if she knew how to get the world to show her a little more respect.

Played-Out (Exhausted) Pleaser Making a go of life, but feeling stressed out, tired, and fatigued. She can't say no, and always has to do the giving in any relationship.

Depressed Pleaser Hurt, miserable, and unhappy, often connected to a loser or womanizer, whom she feels she has to care for and help. (Occupationally, the Depressed Pleaser is often a nurse or other professional care giver.) May need professional help.

Supersuffering Pleaser In real pain, probably has relationship with a misogynist, needs professional help.

Totally Discouraged

To Decide Where to Go, Look Where You've Been

Hopefully, now you have a general idea of who and what a pleaser is and where you fit on the scale. Please keep in mind that no text or quiz is infallible or absolutely precise. A lot depends on the mood you're in when you take the quiz, and on some days you might score higher or lower than on others.

But if you did score somewhere below 80, you probably want to know what you can do about improving your life and achieving a better balance. While being a pleaser can be anything from unfulfilling to painful, you're sure you don't want to become the exact opposite: a controller who causes people pain and dissatisfaction. What's the answer?

We'll get to that answer in good time, but first we need to look at *why* you are a pleaser. What forces molded you into the pleaser you are today? Somebody said, "Know your enemy." Pleasers who know they're getting the raw end of life's deal realize that the enemy is "me."

How well do you know yourself? How acquainted are you with the "little girl" who still lives deep inside you? I often say to clients, "The little girl you once were you still are." Perhaps that doesn't sound too encouraging. Maybe it even rankles a bit. Let's take a look at your child of the past and see what we can learn.

Characteristics of the Pleaser

Following are some basic characteristics of pleaser personalities, depending on your situation and background.

1. Medium to low self-esteem—tendency to think you're not that much, don't really count, don't deserve it, and so forth.
2. Often from family in which emotional needs were unmet, particularly by your father.

32

3. Trying to find, earn, or create as an adult what was missing for you as a child.

4. Daddy's little girl—pleasing him paid off when you were little and you are still trying to please men for the same reasons.

5. A fixer and reformer. You know you can change him.

6. Tendency to fantasize. You don't always grasp reality. Example: "I guess it's okay to live with him and maybe we'll get married later—he's so special."

7. A "controller in reverse." You find someone you can please and then take over the relationship to make it work.

8. Tendency to be "pseudomasochistic." You don't admit it, but you prefer being treated poorly. A nice man would be a total bore.

9. You are quick to blame yourself: "I'm sorry . . . it's my fault . . . how stupid of me. . . ."

10. You have the Avis complex. You can't please him or them but you will "try harder."

11. You are thankful for small favors. Life could be worse. You know he does love you—he gave you a hug after knocking out your tooth.

12. You may be part of the helping and caring professions such as social work, nursing, preschool teaching. You are a care giver at heart.

13. Deep down you feel you don't deserve to be loved or respected.

14. If you have a relationship with God, it is a poor one at best. You see Him as full of wrath and judgment, a "big policeman in the sky" type who is ready to zap you for the slightest infraction or mistake.

The Little Girl
Who Lives in You

"Her heart belongs to Daddy . . ."

When Denise, a pleasant-looking, brown-haired, twenty-one-year-old college junior, came to see me, she was deeply depressed and beginning to feel suicidal. On a scale of one to ten, with ten high, Denise's self-esteem was at minus three. Since age eleven, when she had experienced sex for the first time, she had had, conservatively, one hundred different sexual partners, many for one-night stands, others for a few weeks or months.

Her latest relationship had been especially traumatic and for the first time she had fleeting thoughts of killing herself.

"I think I need a shrink," she said, eyeing me coolly as she took a deep drag on a cigarette. "I heard you talk straight, no bull, so I came."

I told her she was entirely correct and, therefore, would she please observe the NO SMOKING signs all over the office and put out her cigarette.

As Denise's story poured out, it was clear that she was a woman who could not say no—especially to a man. She was trying to fill a gigantic void in her life labeled HEALTHY FATHER IMAGE. Her real father had disappeared when she was three and her mother had gone on to four more marriages. Her mother's fourth husband, a man named John, had seemed to be the father image she was looking for, but she had been unsuccessful in developing any father-daughter relationship with him. He hadn't been interested in Denise or her younger brother and sister, and one of the reasons he had divorced Denise's mother was "not wanting the responsibility of all those kids."

Denise's current stepfather (her mother's fifth husband) was very much at odds with her. They disagreed on just about everything. He was Jewish; she had been raised Methodist. He was a Democrat; she was a member of the Young Republicans on her college campus. He had flashy taste in clothes and cars; she was a traditional preppie.

"We just don't have much respect for each other," Denise observed.

The relationship between Denise and her mother blew from hot to cold almost on a twenty-four-hour cycle. One day they would get along beautifully, the next day they would be fighting and screaming. For example, Denise would call her mother and report her car wasn't working. Her mother would blame Denise for being irresponsible and not having it serviced properly. They would hang up

36

on each other and then one would call the other back later to apologize.

"Mom is always encouraging me to be open and tell her everything," Denise offered. "But when I don't agree with her on something, she screams and yells and we get into a big fight."

But at least Denise had a relationship with her mother and there was love between them. What Denise really wanted was love from a man—something she had never really experienced. Denise wanted love from men so badly she would do anything to get their attention and what she misinterpreted as their affection. The word had gotten out on her college campus that she would go to bed with anybody, and you can bet "anybody" came right over.

All of these young men looked good to Denise. What did she have to compare them to? And so she would make a trade. She would go through all kinds of abuse, degradation, and even sexual perversion to be held, caressed, and told a few nice words. Denise's male friends could treat her like dirt and she would still take them back, take them to bed, and service their sexual needs.

As Denise and I talked, I asked, "How many of these sexual encounters were really fulfilling to you?"

"Fulfilling? What do you mean?" she asked.

"When you went to bed with these men, was it pleasurable? Did you experience an orgasm?"

"I don't know—maybe. I'm not sure I know what one is really like. . . ." Incredible as it may seem, although she had had sexual encounters with more than one hundred partners, some many times, Denise was unsure what it meant to have an orgasm. She was interested, however, in experiencing pleasure, and for her the way to find pleasure was to get a man to hold her, kiss her, and paw her body.

That was all Denise understood about sex. She had no idea it was supposed to be a two-way street. What was important was that the man told her he cared for her. Even on a first date, "I'm crazy about you," and other typical lines were the magic words that prompted her to "go all the way."

Like many pleasers, Denise used a lot of rationalization and denial as her way of smoothing things over. She was particularly skilled in explaining away her repeated episodes with "takers" who simply wanted to use her or "losers" who controlled her by arousing her pity or desire to please.

Denise had an uncanny ability to attract the losers of life because she had suffered such great losses herself. After she lost Daddy at age three, it was all downhill. Her mother couldn't help her because she was busy attracting her own set of losers and digging an ever deeper hole for herself and her daughter. Denise grew up carrying a little girl inside who desperately wanted love and affection, especially from a man.

While some readers of this book will identify with Denise, others will not because their experiences have been much different. But where we can all identify with Denise is in our awareness of the "child of the past" who is deep inside, still affecting our lives in countless ways.

As I mentioned in chapter 1, I often tell the women I counsel, "The little girl you once were you still are." Some clients understand immediately, others are puzzled or even offended. They think they have grown up and left all that behind. But you never leave that little girl behind because she is still there within you. She is always looking for the treatment and experiences she became accustomed to when she was small.

For most of us, that early treatment and those first experiences came from our parents. While I realize there is a great deal of discussion today about mothers and daughters (for example, Nancy Friday's best seller *My Mother, My Self*), I believe that in a very real sense every woman's heart "still belongs to Daddy."

A sizable amount of significant research on the father-daughter relationship has been done by such specialists as Dr. Michael Lamb of the University of Utah. Several popular discussions of daddies and daughters have appeared in recent years, including *Like Father, Like Daughter: How Father Shapes the Woman His Daughter Becomes* by Suzanne Fields, and *Fathers and Daughters* by William S. Appleton, M.D.

Suzanne Fields observes that a girl's first perception of the opposite sex comes from her father. He shapes the daughter's expectations of how a male should behave. Did he hold her hand as she learned to walk? Did he help her struggle through the multiplication tables and fractions? Did he show affection with ease and comfort? Did he hold her close, care how she looked, and notice when she started filling out?[1]

In *Daddy's Girl, Mama's Boy*, coauthors James J. Rue and Louise Shanahan discuss the complex mysteries of how human beings become attracted to one another. People pair off for an almost endless number of reasons and motives, but there is one basic common denominator: We choose a mate who will help us fill the gaps we feel in ourselves. We're trying to complete ourselves sexually, psychologically, aesthetically, and spiritually, and "the parent figure of the opposite sex is our unconscious model for all future romantic encounters."[2]

If a girl grows up in a healthy home, where her father is a stable, loving individual who teaches her that women are to be respected, loved, and cherished, she is lucky. Very few women who have had this kind of childhood ever come to see me. Unfortunately, they have grown up in homes that are far different from the norm.

In Denise's case, Daddy left when she was a very small girl. All she could do was fantasize about what a loving father would be like. She never had one, and she tried to fill that gigantic void by giving herself to men in exchange for a few scraps of warmth and attention.

Mary Made Excuses for Bill's Affairs

In other cases, Daddy doesn't leave but he never provides the affection his little girl needs. So she grows up and gets married, as Mary did to Bill, the construction company president. Mary, a petite brunette with a dimpled smile and nervous hands, was very much a pleaser, someone who was trying to find someone powerful who could provide the love and care her father had never shown.

Bill seemed to be a perfect choice. He was good at putting things together, a powerful doer, an action-oriented man. Bill could make things happen and his very insecure, pleasing wife was drawn to him like a moth to a flame. Mary felt she just couldn't make it on her own. She needed the support and strength of someone like Bill.

It turned out that Bill needed her, too. Mary was soon saddled with three small children as well as a part-time job as a bookkeeper in her husband's company. Mary was supposed to save the company money, but Bill never gave her any of her own to spend. She had to account for every penny, whether at home or at work.

Bill saw no problem, however, with the way *he* spent money. He bought a lot of personal toys for himself as well as making major purchases for the entire family: widescreen

TV sets, VCRs, and ATCs, for himself and all the kids. It knocked the family budget for a loop, but Mary was always understanding. She was a pleaser and she made excuses to keep things running smoothly.

Mary was such a pleaser that she even made excuses for Bill's affairs with other women. I listened a bit incredulously as Mary rationalized his behavior.

"Well, I know by the end of the day I'm so exhausted I don't have the time and energy for him sexually," she said. "I understand why he takes secretaries and real estate agents to bed."

As Mary and I talked, it became quite clear why she was putting up with Bill and his controlling abuse. Her mother had endured all kinds of abuse from her father, a man who never treated his wife or children with any affection. It isn't correct to say Mary's father wasn't a key person in her life. He was a *very* key person, but his influence was almost all negative.

In chapter 1 I mentioned that the theme of the poor daddy-daughter relationship would be coming up again and again. I am ready to say that the most profound relationship in the family is between daddy and daughter. In his book *Fathers and Daughters*, William Appleton writes:

It is surprising that fathers affect their daughters' femininity more than their sons' masculinity. Researchers, theorists, and my own clinical and research experiences all concur that a good relationship with a warm and accepting father who is not too frightened of her sexuality is extremely important to a little girl. Someone who can enjoy her beauty, her smile, her pretty dress, her first efforts at makeup and jewelry, helps her gain the confidence that she can attract, charm and interest a man.[3]

In Mary's case, her father never affirmed her in anything she ever did, from band in junior high to cheerleading in high school. She always felt as if she never had or deserved her daddy's love.

So whom did Mary find for a husband? She managed to "attract a man," but the wrong kind. She married a man she could "count on"—one she knew would never give her all of his love, just as her father had not. The familiar is easier to handle than the unfamiliar, even when it's painful.

When Mary Changed the Locks, Bill Went Berserk

But even Mary had her limits. The situation came to a head when she discovered Bill was having an affair with her younger sister, Jeannine, who had a husband as well. Even pleasers like Mary have a limit when that last straw snaps. As soon as she heard the news, she went home, put all of Bill's clothes and other belongings in the garage, and had the locks changed on the house.

When Bill came home at eleven o'clock that night, he found that his key did not work in the lock. At first he thought it might be those several beers he had hoisted before heading home. But once it dawned on him that the lock had been changed, he went berserk. He literally tore the door off the house and frightened Mary so badly that she called the police to restrain him.

I'd like to say that once Mary decided to use action instead of pacifying words and pleasing excuses, Bill shaped up. But that was not to be. This marriage did not make it, but I am happy to report that Mary will. The last time I talked with her, she was making plans to get some training at a community college and to start life over for herself at age thirty-one. With three small children, she knows it won't be easy. She will have to claw and scratch to make a better life for herself and them. But far better that she claw and scratch than simply lie down and let life continue to kick her in the teeth.

Time and again I find myself saying, especially to pleasing women, "All right, life has kicked you squarely in the teeth. You have been treated unfairly, abused, and taken advantage of. Now the question is, what are you going to do about it?"

When a pleaser can understand that she lives in a world of controllers and that she must stand up to those controllers, then, and only then, can she start finding the happiness and fulfillment she has always been missing.

You Can't Change Your Grain, but You Can Change

When I urge pleasers who have been cheated, abused, controlled, bullied, and manipulated for most of their lives to do something about it, I am not suggesting that they simply "grow up" and get rid of the "little girl" they have been carrying inside all these years. A lot of self-help and pop psychology books say you can change and become a "new you." *I'm sorry, but you can't become a new you. You can change the way you act, but you can't change who and what you are.*

Like the grain in a piece of wood, your basic temperament and personality is there for life. You can shape it, sand it, paint it, varnish it, and polish it, but the grain will not change.

When we use the old cliché "That goes against my grain," we are saying that something or someone is totally at odds with how we see life. In some of my other books, I described how each of us learns during childhood "a style of life" by accepting certain "life lines" as true for us. These

43

lines all begin with the words "I only count when I. . . ." Some typical life lines for the pleasers I counsel include the following:

- I only count when I keep everything smooth and on an even keel.
- I only count when I make everyone happy.
- I only count when everyone likes me.
- I only count when everyone approves of what I do.
- I only count when I do a perfect job.
- I only count when I can care for others.
- I only count when I suffer for the sake of others.

How do we learn these life lines that determine the grain of the personalities we carry with us throughout life? In our earliest years, our parents give the most important input. Depending on our family situation, Grandma and Grandpa might have a great deal to say, or it might be a favorite aunt or uncle.

Later on, teachers, coaches, schoolmates, and friends put the finishing touches on our style of life. By the time we are in high school, our life lines are firmly established. We have learned that we only count when we do and say certain things that seem to fit us. We only count when and if we operate in certain basic ways. We have come to terms with our world.

As we carry our life lines and life-styles right on into adulthood, we bring along that same little child who learned those life lines in the first place. Many therapists and counselors call this little boy or girl the "inner child of the past," a term coined by Dr. W. Hugh Missildine in his work with the Children's Mental Health Center in Columbus, Ohio.

Missildine, a child psychologist and teacher of psychiatry at the university level, used three basic principles:

1. Your inner child of the past still exists and affects your life as an adult.
2. You have to learn how to be a parent to the little boy or girl who is still inside of you. That little boy or girl may not like being parented, but if you don't get firm with your inner child, he or she will rule the roost.
3. Mutual respect is the only way to get along with your inner child, as well as with anyone else. (This is an excellent point for pleasers, who usually live without receiving mutual respect from spouses, children, friends, and others.)

What Were Your Parents Like?

Hugh Missildine believes we are shaped by several kinds of parent personalities. These include the following:

The *flaw pickers* are perfectionistic parents who are strong on discipline, performance, and criticism. Perfectionistic parents don't necessarily spank or even scold in a loud voice. Instead they say, "Sit up straight, dear. Men don't like a girl with poor posture." Or, "Yes, honey, that is a pretty dress, but I really think you ought to wear the gray one to the party."

The flaw-picking parent makes everything the child is and does a matter of endless concern. The result is that the child grows into adulthood, taking along an inner child of the past who is always whispering, "You *can* do better, you *should* do better, you *ought* to do better, you *aren't up to standard*." More often than not, suicidal teenagers have flaw-picking parents.

The *drill sergeant* is the authoritarian and overcoercive parent who is always on the child's back, always barking orders and commands.

"Get up, let's get going. . . . Did you brush your teeth? . . . Dinner's getting cold. . . . Did you do your homework? . . . Don't mumble. . . . Don't talk with your mouth full. . . . No TV until homework is done. . . . It's bedtime, no exceptions, you need your sleep! . . . How do you expect to grow up to be big and strong? Now finish your carrots!"

Children raised by overcoercive parents often develop what is called a "resistant life-style" cycle. Instead of running faster and hurrying more, they slow down. They stall and dawdle. They take this attitude into adulthood and their inner child of the past is always telling them, "You don't have to take this. . . . Don't let them push you around. . . . Okay, you need the job, but just wait. . . . You can do it in a minute, what's the hurry? . . ."

The *wimps* are the overpermissive and oversubmissive parents who let their child rule the roost. The child parented by the oversubmissive father or mother hears comments like these:

"Oh, I guess you can go if you want to. . . . Well, if you want to stay up a little longer, that's okay. . . . I don't understand why these teachers make you do all this homework. . . . Okay, okay, if you don't like peas you don't have to eat peas. Just leave them on your plate."

Adults who were reared by overpermissive and submissive parents develop an inner child of the past who is very demanding and hard to get along with. Pleasers are seldom developed by oversubmissive parents, who are far more likely to develop controllers who want their way, have explosive tempers, and indulge themselves in whatever they think they need to be happy. If this kind of person does develop any pleasing characteristics, they are usually manipulative in nature. She will "please" to get her way, but if her husband or friends cross her, look out!

Mr. and Mrs. Santa Claus are the overindulgent parents who are first cousins to those who are oversubmissive and permissive. This kind of parenting can produce a "daddy's little girl" who often hears:

"Would you like to have that? Let's get it right now. . . . What a wonderful report card! Three Bs and an A. What would you like as a special treat? . . . It's okay if you flunked math—these days you can get by with calculators."

The child raised by indulgent parents becomes an adult who is often bored, listless, and incapable of finishing what has been started. Her little girl from the past tells her, "You deserve better than you're getting in this lousy job. . . . Your roommate [husband] is unreasonable for wanting you to do so much. . . . People are boring—why aren't they more interested in *you?*"

The *wicked stepmother* kind of parents are the ones who are punitive toward their children. The child raised in this kind of home hears, "You're no good. . . . You'll never amount to anything. . . . Why are you such a devil? . . . You're sloppy. . . . You're lazy. . . . Can't you do anything right?"

Accompanying all this verbal abuse is plenty of physical abuse: slaps, paddlings, beatings. The child reared in this kind of atmosphere grows into an adult whose inner child of the past motivates her with guilt and fear. This badly treated inner child constantly suggests possible ways to get revenge, to get back at anyone who may be in a position of authority.

It is sometimes difficult to understand why an adult might act so childish, but an adult raised by a "wicked stepmother" could have her inner child whispering, "Okay, if he has the right to punish me, then I have the right to punish him." Because the inner child wants to strike back at the authority figure, so does the adult if the adult lets the inner child do the controlling.

The adult who looks back to a punitive childhood can't trust anyone. She is always afraid. She may become a pleaser out of fear and guilt and spend her life in martyrlike self-belittlement. I've often counseled women who will purchase a new blouse or sweater, take it home, hang it in the closet for a few days, then take it back to the store, pleading that they "just can't afford it." Actually, they believe they just don't deserve it, and they simply cannot keep their purchase and enjoy it in any way.

Chronically AWOL is my label for neglectful parents who check out on their children in one way or another. Sometimes parents become absentees through extreme circumstances they cannot control: death, divorce, a job that forces long separations. In many cases, however, a parent lives in the home with the child but is really "absent" as far as being interested in the child in any real sense.

The child reared by neglectful parents often hears remarks like these: "I'm busy, don't bother me. . . . I can't help you with your homework, I've got to make these calls. . . . What was that? Whatever you think, I really don't have time to talk now."

Neglectful parents seldom, if ever, share feelings. They just can't be bothered. They are cut off from their children, who are then forced to grow up "on their own," psychologically speaking.

The child raised by the neglectful "absentee" parent grows into an adult whose child of the past keeps warning her about becoming closely attached to anyone. The woman becomes a pleaser who may use her pleasing ways to exploit others to get the love, affection, attention, and support she missed as a little girl. At the worst extreme, the neglected girl might become a prostitute. In Denise's case, she was neglected as a little girl and wound up sleeping with any boy who came along. One of the few differences between Denise and a prostitute was that prostitutes get paid a fee. Denise collected her "pay" by getting any form of attention she could.

"Out of my life" best describes the rejecting parent who literally refuses to accept a child in any way. In her autobiography *Thursday's Child*, Eartha Kitt tells a classic tale of being rejected by her mother and new husband. Eartha's mother had been deserted by Eartha's father and when she remarried, her second husband demanded that she turn Eartha over to relatives so they could have an "unencumbered" life of their own.

But Eartha's relatives didn't want her either, and she grew up feeling she was a burden, no good, and the target of abuse and scorn.

It is not surprising that Eartha Kitt became a "pleaser" who turned to entertainment to gain the acceptance and approval she never had as a child. The adult who was rejected as a child hears that child of the past constantly whispering, "There must be something wrong with you. . . . You aren't really lovable. . . . You have to earn approval and prove that you are valuable. . . . Don't believe him; he says he loves you but he'll probably leave you sooner or later. . . ."

The woman who was rejected as a little girl will often seek security in place of love. She will often be a loner whose few friends see her as self-centered and easily hurt. She may be known as an "arm's-length person."

The above quick sketches give several basic parenting styles that determine the life lines we eventually accept as truth and keep telling ourselves all our lives. Do you constantly find yourself saying, in one way or another, "I only count when I do a *really good* job"? It's likely your parents were perfectionists.

Are you a procrastinator? Are you usually late? Do you find yourself saying, "I don't have to hurry—let them wait"? It's quite likely you had authoritarian parents who put a lot of pressure on you.

Do you find yourself saying, "I don't know why he can't see it my way; maybe it isn't worth trying to stay in this relationship"? Chances are excellent your parents were permissive or perhaps too indulgent. In a word, they spoiled you, and now the little girl inside is deciding that she wants to pick up her marbles and go home.

Are you a loner? Are your best friends books? Or, if you are athletic, do you prefer individual sports such as jogging or bicycling? Perhaps you find yourself saying, "I don't trust him, and I wish he'd stop acting so bossy, but what can I expect? Why would anybody really want to love me?"

If you show any of the above behaviors, more than likely you are a child from a punitive, neglectful, or rejecting situation. You have been abused physically and/or verbally, and in some cases, ignored totally or simply abandoned and handed on to someone else by parents who wanted nothing to do with you. It is no wonder you feel worthless and incapable of really trusting or loving anyone else completely. You were never loved as a child, and you can't believe anybody would really want to love you now.

What Do You Do with That Little Girl Inside?

I realize it can be a bit frightening to be told you can't change who you really are. My counseling case load includes many people who have been reared to have strong religious convictions or who have had a "born again" experience and have placed their faith in Christ. Conservative Christian teaching often emphasizes becoming "a completely new person" and that "the old has gone and the new has come."[4]

And there is also the often-quoted line from the love chapter—1 Corinthians 13—in which Paul says, "When I was a child, I talked like a child, I thought like a child, I reasoned like a child. When I became a man, I put childish ways behind me."[5]

It is possible to quote verses like these and claim that the "inner child of the past" is so much psychological gobbledygook.

But I have talked to enough patients who have been reared in Christian homes and who have established their own Christian homes to know even the most sincere believer does not magically change. The grain of the wood is set, and everyone struggles with his or her own grain throughout life. No one is perfect or totally mature.

When Paul says a believer in Christ is "a new creation," I believe he means that now this person has new choices and responsibilities to live life according to the teachings and power promised through a new and dynamic relationship to God. You can, and should, put away "childish behavior," but you can't get rid of your inner child—that little girl who will always be part of you. Here is what you must do with your inner child:

Accept that little girl inside. Admit she is there and that she plays a key role in how you feel and what you think—your very perception of life. When you say, "I only count when I achieve and please others," that's your inner child talking. Remember, you learned your "I only count when . . ." life lines back in your childhood, not as an adult.

Set limits for that little girl inside. That little girl is part of you, but *only part.* You are now an adult and you are in charge—if you want to be. You can't change the grain of your wood, but you can change your attitude. Above all, you can change how you act when something "goes against your grain"—when your inner child starts to fret, fume, and throw a tantrum.

The key principles for parenting the little girl inside of you are the same ones you should use in parenting your children. Use firm but loving guidelines as you discipline your child of the past the same way you discipline your three-year-old son or daughter:

Don't belittle or bully your inner child, and don't let the child do the same to you.

Don't punish your little girl within. Instead, seek to discipline, train, and teach her. You can use many of the same Reality Discipline principles I recommend when counseling parents on child rearing. In my books, films, and seminars I explain how Reality Discipline makes children accountable and responsible for their actions.

I believe you can make your inner child accountable and responsible too. The process of maturity—growing up to be a whole adult—is to accept the "little girl" feelings you have deep inside. Respect these feelings, but don't be dominated by them. Learn to live with them, but on your (adult) terms.

Keep in mind the sage wisdom of the person who said, "You can only be a child once, but you can be immature forever." If you let that little girl inside of you run things, you will remain immature all your life. I often tell my patients, "You can't just follow your feelings . . . you must use your head and discipline yourself cognitively—with your thoughts."

The rest of this book will be devoted to helping you use cognitive self-discipline to handle that little girl inside of you—especially the little pleaser who is either trying to manipulate life or is finding herself manipulated and mistreated by life instead.

The difference between Reality Discipline and cognitive self-discipline is that Reality Discipline is a system for children (see my book *Making Children Mind without Losing Yours*). Cognitive self-discipline is a system for adults —especially pleasers.

How to Start Working with the Little Girl Inside

Are you a product of a home where there was a lot of perfectionism, bossing, and authoritarian rule and behavior? Then the first thing you ought to do is watch for the times you start making demands on yourself. Take smaller bites of life. Perfectionism is slow suicide. It's time to tell that little girl inside you simply can't please everyone.

Do you come from a home where there was a lot of punitive behavior and abuse, both physical and verbal? What you need to do is be more kind to yourself. Your tendency will be to talk to yourself in punishing and abusive ways:

"Can't you ever learn, you idiot?"

"You never say the right thing in front of others."

"You're a failure—who wants to bother with you?"

"You'll never amount to anything."

"Why do you always make such a fool of yourself?"

Make a conscious effort to let your little girl inside know that this kind of talk won't do. Tell yourself you are learning, you are valuable, and you are loved. Don't even use terms such as "I am *not* stupid," which still keeps planting negative ideas in your mind. Say instead, "I can handle this," or, "That was great—more like the real me."

Always talk about your good points, your strengths, and where you know you are achieving and growing. Practice the power of being a positive pleaser and try to please yourself for a change.

Did you come from an overindulgent home, or were your parents overly permissive? Maybe you find yourself trying to play the role of the manipulator. You may try to please your husband or your friends, but only to a point. If they cross you, you explode and literally throw tantrums of one kind or another. What you need to do is make more demands on yourself. Set limits on your impulsive nature. Above all, make a conscious effort to respect the rights and feelings of others.

Did you come from a home where you were neglected or even rejected? Did your father, in particular, pay little attention to you? Did he check out or become absent for one reason or another? Do you now find yourself married to a man who is acting the same way?

I counsel many women who grew up in malfunctioning homes where they had very negative impressions of what men are supposed to be like. Their fathers deserted them, abused them, or simply failed to communicate any warmth and affection. Incredibly, they seem to have found the very same kind of man for a husband. It's almost as if they decide they don't deserve anything else. Besides, this is familiar and more comfortable.

In other cases, the woman is a victim of a terrible paradox. She swears she will escape the father image she learned to despise as a child. She will never marry a man who even faintly resembles her father. But what she does not understand is that Daddy's indelible imprint is not so easily washed out of his daughter. In many cases, she does wind up with a man who has many of her father's characteristics—*or who seems to develop them later*. Only with maturity does a woman understand her need for a husband who is similar to her father. By then it is often too late.

What can you do if you are married to this kind of man— someone who is neglecting and even rejecting? We'll talk about that in part 3, but for now remember that you can at least do little kindnesses for yourself. Do a little indulging of yourself when you can and, above all, absolutely refuse to buy into the critical abuse you are hearing from your spouse. This is his way of controlling, dominating, and crushing you to fulfill his own sick needs.

Do not engage in self-criticism. Tell yourself, "I am special. I have no need to be perfect or to prove my value. The grain of my wood is set, but it's a beautiful grain and I am proud of it!"

Because I strongly emphasize the need to develop the spiritual aspect of life along with the mental, physical, and emotional sides, I am convinced that self-image is really a matter of faith. If you truly believe you are a creation of God—you are an *original*—there is a tremendous amount of comfort and support in that realization.

This chapter gives you what I call half the story on "why you are the way you are"—why you resort to pleasing behavior of one kind or another. The other half of who you are lies in your birth order—where you fit on your family tree. Your birth order can tell you a great deal about yourself and your pleasing or not-so-pleasing ways. Are you an only child or first born? That can easily account for your perfectionism and why you are constantly trying to please the world by achieving standards that always seem just out of reach.

Are you a middle child? That could explain why you are always trying to mediate and be the peacemaker.

Are you a baby of the family? You, too, have your ways of being a pleaser, but you're quite clever and devious about it.

Only child, first born, middle child, or baby—whatever you are has a lot to do with the kind of little girl you're carrying around inside today. I'll show you why in the next chapter.

3

Why a Pleaser
Can Be Born Anytime

HE: "You look lovely tonight . . . what's your birth order?"
SHE: "I'm sorry, I never get intimate on the first date."

One of my favorite counseling tools is "birth order": the
limb on which you are born into your family tree. Alfred
Adler, who founded the "school" of psychology in which
I got my training, once said, "We have often drawn attention to the fact that, before we can judge a human being,
we must know the situation in which he grew up. An important moment is the position which the child occupied
in his family constellation."[1]

After twenty years of work in counseling and psychotherapy, I have learned the wisdom of Adler's words. When he talks about "judging" people, he really means understanding them. And one of the best ways to understand them is to "recognize whether an individual is a first born, an only child, the youngest child, or the like."[2]

If we do a quick sketch of the major levels of birth order, we find the following characteristics:

Only children and *first borns* usually are perfectionistic, reliable, conscientious, list makers, well organized, critical, serious, and scholarly. They are also eager to please, goal oriented, and respectful of authority. The difference between the only child and the first born is typically one of degree. The only child is *super*perfectionistic, *super*realistic, and so on.

Middle children tend to be mediators, avoiders of conflict, and independent. They show extreme loyalty to their peer group and have many friends. Another characteristic that strikes a chord with middle children at birth-order seminars is that they have the fewest pictures in the family photo album!

Last borns or "babies" of the family characteristically prove to be manipulative, charming, able to easily blame others, good at showing off, people persons, good in sales, precocious, engaging.

If we had to choose from the above four groups (I put only children and first borns in separate categories), where do you think we would find the most pleasers? Generally speaking, you find more pleasers among only children and first borns, but that doesn't mean you can't find pleaser personalities of different kinds in all major birth order levels. Let me show you why.

How Can Goal-Oriented First Borns Become Pleasers?

At first glance, only children and first borns don't seem to fit the pleaser mold because they are so goal oriented (aggressive). A major trait of many only children and first borns is the tendency to take charge, get things organized, and "make it happen." As I mentioned in *The Birth Order Book*, a favorite exercise I use in birth-order workshops is to divide the crowd into four groups. Only children go to one corner, first borns to another, middle children to a third corner, and the last borns (those precocious babies of the family) are put in the far corner where I hope they won't make too much of a ruckus.

I don't give many instructions. I simply tell the groups to chat and get to know one another. Then I move around the room, joining each group and chatting briefly. Before I leave the group, I try to unobtrusively leave a slip of paper facedown on the floor. When I finish my tour of the four groups, each one has that piece of paper left under the feet of the participants, who still have been given no formal instructions as to what to do next. Each piece of paper reads as follows:

Congratulations! You are the leader of this group. Please introduce yourself to the rest of this group, and then have each person do the same. As you talk together, make a list of personality characteristics you all seem to share. Be prepared to report back to the rest of the seminar with your "composite picture" of yourselves. Please start work immediately.

I have done this exercise with over two hundred different groups and it's always fascinating to watch birth order take its natural course. Almost always, someone in the group of only children or first borns will be first to stoop and pick up the paper. Usually the middle children follow, and soon all three of these groups are hard at work on their assignment.

And the last-born babies? Quite often, they keep milling around while the piece of paper remains on the floor unread.

I wait a minute or two and then announce, "You have only two minutes to finish your assignment. We'll hear your report at the end of that time!"

I can almost see the only children and first borns jump as they redouble their efforts to finish. The middle children are a little more laid back but they, too, keep at it. As for the last borns, in many cases they're having such a great time they never even hear what I say.

I'll never forget one seminar where the babies milled around in a far corner, having a great time chattering and getting to know one another. But nobody was writing down any "characteristics of everyone in the group." That's because they had never read the piece of paper, which wound up under the feet of one particularly jovial gentleman who probably was the top salesman in his firm.

If you're the baby of your family, please don't take offense. I'm not making fun of last borns, because I'm a last born myself. I tell the story to illustrate the businesslike, "let's get to it" conscientious nature of only children and first borns. Remember their characteristics? Perfectionistic, reliable, conscientious, list makers, well organized, critical, serious, and scholarly. You could also add to that list goal oriented, achiever, self-sacrificing, conservative, supporter of law and order, believer in authority and ritual, legalistic, loyal, and self-reliant.

What makes the only child or first born run down such a straight and narrow path? There are at least two good reasons:

1. *The first born is Mom and Dad's first effort at the mysterious art of parenting.* Many brand-new parents have a paradoxical way of raising little Gladys. Part of them says they should be protective, anxious, tentative, and inconsistent. The other part says, "Be strict, raise this child right." If you're a first born, you'll just have to accept reality. To be blunt about it, Mom and Dad practiced on you! The result was that you were often subject to demands, being pushed and encouraged toward more and better performance.

   If parents want to be honest, their first-born child is an experiment. Everything little Gladys does—negative or positive—is a major event. And most of it gets recorded on slides, color prints, or videocassettes.

2. *With all of this responsibility weighing heavily on their shoulders, first borns often turn out quite serious.* I've often thought that it's no wonder research shows first borns walk and talk earlier than anyone else in the family. With all that attention and expectation from the adults, they probably do it in self-defense.

   First borns learn early to make things happen, and they like to know what's happening to them and when. They aren't much for surprises. They love being organized, on time, and "stable."

Remember, first borns look up and see no one but Mom and Dad. There are no older brothers and sisters ahead of them from whom to learn. They have to learn from those gigantic paragons of seeming perfection: Mommy and Daddy,

Grandma and Grandpa, and other adults. First borns could easily be called "little adults" who go on to their destiny—to be the leaders and achievers in society. It is no surprise that out of the first twenty-three astronauts into space, twenty-one were first borns. Studies show that first borns get the highest S.A.T. scores, and are likely to become Rhodes scholars and even presidents of the United States.

What about the only child? At the risk of blanket labels, you can simply add "super" or "ultra" to all first-born characteristics, and you have the only child. I often say the one person who can make a first born look easygoing is an only child.

"Lonely onlies" often come across as confident, competent, and in complete control of a situation, but don't let that fool you. The only child is almost always a superperfectionist who can never run fast enough or straight enough or far enough to meet his or her extra-high standards. Because the high-jump bar of life is always just out of reach, the only child often feels a deep sense of inferiority. Only children may come on strong, but they do it to hide their greatest weakness—feeling as if they don't really measure up.

First Borns Split into Two Camps

So how do we find a pleaser in all this first-born, goal-oriented behavior, assertiveness, and achievement? It's quite simple, really, because no personality theory freezes people in a concrete mold. Only children and first borns can divide into two basic types: compliant and strong willed. Or to put it in even simpler terms, timid and assertive.

Compliant only children and first borns are the reliable, obedient types who always say, "Yes, Mom. . . . Okay, Dad. . . . Sure, I'll do it."

First borns and only children tend to be good in school and reliable, conscientious employees. Perhaps the key to why compliant first borns run so fast and so straight in life is their need for approval. First they're out to please Mom and Dad, then they want to please their employers, teachers, coaches, friends, and eventually their spouses and their own children.

The Compliant First Born versus the Used Sushi

I've done a lot of research with first borns, and most of my counseling load is with first borns and only children. Perhaps my best research is done at home because I am married to Sande, a compliant, pleasing first born if I ever saw one. I have often shared the story of Sande's encounter with a piece of half-poached salmon in one of the country's finest restaurants. She kept picking at it but not really eating much. After several anxious inquiries from me, she admitted it was "not quite done in the middle."

"Not quite done" didn't really describe it. It was really a candidate for somebody's used-sushi bar. I quickly called the waiter over and informed him of the problem. Horrified, he swept Sande's plate off the table and vanished into the kitchen, where the chef was soon doubly horrified. In a few minutes, a new plate of poached salmon, thoroughly done in the middle and everywhere else, arrived, followed later by a huge baked Alaska dessert, compliments of the chagrined and apologetic house.

Sande enjoyed her second salmon dinner, which was cooked to perfection, but she was still a bit embarrassed by the whole incident. A compliant and pleasing first born, she would have preferred not to complain but to just "bear with it." Sande has always been patient, nurturing, and care giving. What she has managed to escape, however, is the trap of the discouraged perfectionist, who is often an only child or first born.

Come to think of it, Sande is a classic illustration of what I call the Positive Pleaser—someone who has come to terms with her pleasing personality and lives in happy fulfillment. We'll be hearing more about Sande in the last chapter of this book, where I'll tell how pleasers can find happiness in a controlling world.

And it is a controlling world out there. In fact, in my counseling I often find pleasing wives married to controlling husbands. And more often than not, both are only children or first borns—one of the most volatile combinations you can find for marriage. The compliant first-born wives usually take it on the psychological chin from their first-born controller husbands, who prove to be miserly with everything from money to affection to time with their families. They go for years being walked on, nursing resentment quietly, but when they do blow, they usually make it a decisive production.

> DR. LEMAN: "What do you want?"
> AUDREY: "Out!"

Audrey and Frank are a couple who fit this description perfectly. Frank, the first-born controller, had driven Audrey, the only-child pleaser, to the brink. She had suffered silently, through nine years and five children, while living with Frank's black-and-white engineer's mentality. Audrey had to account for every nickel in the family budget and had to raise their five children, ages nine down to eighteen months, alone. Frank simply wasn't there. If business appointments for his high-tech aerospace firm didn't keep him out nights, his participation in city league sports did. In the summer it was softball, in the winter, basketball. He was gone at least five out of seven evenings and the other two found him collapsing in front of the TV set, not wanting to be bothered with mundane family matters.

When I asked Audrey what she wanted, she said, "Out." Audrey had had it. She lived in a fairly small community where she hadn't been able to make many friends. She felt trapped and isolated. She had tried to please Frank and the children and gotten very little in return. She felt ignored and, while Frank didn't physically abuse her in any way, his nit-picking engineer's nature often let her know that she didn't quite measure up to what he had in mind for a wife. Actually, "housekeeper" would probably have fit Frank's concept of a wife better. He had, in effect, abandoned Audrey and buried himself in his own world.

Fortunately, I got Audrey to see that wanting out was no solution. She would still have to deal with the children and work out visitation rights with Frank, and also have to cope with making a living when she had no marketable skills. As for Frank, all he needed was a little bringing up short with a proper approach. He didn't really understand what being a nurturing and care-giving husband is about. His own parents had been perfectionists who raised him to toe the mark and then get out there and make one of his own. Wasn't that what life was all about?

As is often the case, sex had been put on hold between Frank and Audrey and, while he was not chasing other women, he was burying himself in work and activities.

"You've been trying to please Frank," I told Audrey, "but not in all the right ways. Try approaching him sexually and see what happens."

What Audrey didn't realize was that she and Frank had different "love languages." Men tend to show their love through sex and providing for their families. Admiration and respect are important to them. Somewhere near the bottom of the list are communication and touching. Women, however, place communication and emotional intimacy first. This is why it is so important for spouses to get behind each other's eyes and see how the other person views life. Cognitive self-discipline can be a help in making a conscious effort to please one's mate.

As for Frank, I told him that his wife had been trying to do most of the pleasing in their family. Now what was *he* going to try to do? Frank got my point and started spending more time at home. He didn't work late as much and cut his sports activities in half.

Strangely enough, the simplistic solution of "each trying to please the other a bit more" worked in this case. Fortunately, Audrey came to me before the marriage had totally disintegrated.

Audrey thought she wasn't that interested in sex, but like a dutiful first born, she decided to do what she was assigned to do. As their sexual relationship was rekindled, Audrey and Frank started talking about feelings, and Frank saw the error of his controlling ways. As he became more attentive to Audrey, she felt more attracted toward him. Sex wasn't a duty; it became enjoyable for the first time.

Mabel Was a Played-Out Perfectionist

Before counseling, Audrey had been well on her way to becoming a "discouraged perfectionist," a problem I see in many first borns and only children. I think especially of Mabel, thirty-seven, mother of three, who ran her own dress shop as well as trying to keep a taxi service going for her three girls, who were members of every dance class, Brownie troop, and pony softball team in town. On the pleaser hierarchy (*see* chapter 1), Mabel fit perfectly at the "played out" level. Her perfectionism and desire to "do it all" had driven her to the edge of Bonkersdom.

Whenever I suspect I'm talking to a discouraged perfectionist, I give her a simple test in which she compares her real self to her ideal self. With Mabel the results were predictable. Ideally, she wanted to be organized and efficient, but in reality her business was in a financial shambles. She had a flair for design and displays, but her books were an accountant's nightmare.

Ideally, Mabel wanted to use her time wisely, but in reality she was always scheduling too much, running behind, and always late. Instead of steadily progressing toward her goals, she procrastinated, put things off to the last minute, and tried to get everything done in an incredible flurry of activity that left everyone worn out, run down, and turned off.

Time wasn't the only area where Mabel had unrealistic expectations. She wanted her marriage to be romantic— "just the way it was before we were married." She wanted to be beautiful, sexually aggressive, and expressive. In reality, however, what sex she and her husband, George, did have was mechanical and brief.

Mabel wanted to feel beautiful on the inside and able to take care of everyone, everything, and "do it all." The real Mabel, however, was frustrated, angry, and just plain tired.

Above all, Mabel wanted to feel self-assured, confident, and secure. The real Mabel had to see that she was a super-pleaser because she needed the approval of others. *Mabel needed to be needed.*

I was able to help Mabel, but only after she learned to say no, first to herself and then to others who kept putting pressure on her. Once she got her time under better control, life was less hectic for everyone. Perfectionistic first-born pleasers like Mabel need to realize that perfectionism is not an attribute but a hang-up. Men often use perfectionism as a way of being the best at whatever they try. Women, however, will use perfectionism as a way to avoid criticism, to please, and to gain approval.

If there is anything a perfectionist pleaser needs to work on it is not putting herself down when others criticize. Recognize that you are sensitive. That's part of the little girl inside still trying to get approval from critical parents or maybe a critical teacher.

When you hear criticism, your natural reaction is to start criticizing yourself and admitting, "He's right . . . they're right . . . I blew it again. Why can't I ever get it right?"

Perfectionistic pleasers tend to be pessimists. They see the glass half empty instead of half full. In fact, they actually prefer situations that need fixing or "filling up." If they goof on doing all this fixing and filling, it eats at them like corrosive acid. A good bumper sticker for a perfectionistic pleaser would read: ONE MISTAKE CAN RUIN MY WHOLE DAY!

If you suspect you may be in the perfectionistic-pleaser category, try this kind of self-talk the next time you blow it: "Mistakes happen. I give my little girl inside permission to make some mistakes. What is the worst that can happen because I made a mistake? Nobody's perfect—why should I try to be the first one who ever was?"

When mistakes happen or things go wrong, don't dwell on them. Try seeing the glass half full. Think of two or three good things that happened earlier that day or even last week.

We'll talk more about ways to control perfectionism in later chapters, especially chapter 6. For now, here is one more key thought for anyone who suspects she might be a compliant but perfectionistic first-born pleaser: Remember to practice forgiveness. Whenever we hear the word *forgiveness*, we immediately think of all the times we should forgive others. Sunday-school lessons about forgiving "seventy times seven" may come to mind. Forgiving others is a much needed practice and skill, but forgiving yourself is even more important. You should forgive yourself *seven hundred times seven*. In fact, if you can't forgive yourself for your mistakes and shortcomings, it is doubtful that you can ever totally succeed in forgiving someone else.

Middle-Born Pleasers Keep Things Smooth

To understand middle-born children, you must remember one thing: They seldom take after their older brother or sister, and are often "as different as night and day." Whatever the middle child becomes depends on her perception of her first-born brother or sister. Along with the style of parenting she receives (discussed in chapter 2), her style of life is developed by the way she "bounces off" the first born in the family.

If the first born is compliant and pleasing, the middle child might be a manipulator or a controller. If the first born comes on strong, the middle child can wind up a victim, a martyr, or a good old-fashioned pleaser who simply tries to avoid trouble and keep peace.

All research studies on birth order come to the same general conclusion on second-born children—they are quite likely to be the opposite of first borns.

That's why it's not wise to label all middle borns as pleasers who aren't looking for trouble. Some middle borns can be impatient, easily frustrated, very competitive, rebels, aggressive scrappers, and family goats. Other middle borns turn out sociable, friendly, outgoing, and have a lot of friends. They take life in stride with a laid-back, easygoing air. They're not that competitive, they make great peacemakers and mediators, and *they're always interested in avoiding conflict.* I have never done a study, but it's my guess that many of the ambassadors and diplomats throughout the world are middle borns who love their profession of avoiding conflict and handling disagreements.

If you are a middle child who finds herself trying to please and "smooth out" a controlling and chaotic world, read on to understand why. Some general descriptions of middle children include the following:

1. *The middle child feels the squeeze from both directions.* In the typical three-child family, the first born is usually the achieving "big cheese" and the last-born baby is the attention-getting little clown or charmer. The middle child, however, doesn't get as much attention and often winds up feeling left out, neglected, and, to put it in more adult terms, "without much respect."

   One way I can almost always get a laugh in a birth order seminar is to say to all middle borns in the audience: "Family photo album." They look blank for a minute and then they start to chuckle. They realize that there are several hundred pictures of the first born and almost as many of the baby, but for some strange reason very few pictures of them.

2. *Because they are "fifth wheels," middle borns often go outside the family circle to get respect and attention.* Friends and social activities are normally very important to the middle born. To avoid the pain and frustration of being an "outsider" in the family, the middle child usually leaves home the quickest. I don't mean that he or she moves out, but middle children are often over at friends' houses, or are the first ones to start dating and attending parties.

3. *Middle-born children are known for "playing it closer to the vest" than the other birth orders.* By this I mean they are often quite secretive. Ironically enough, while they have a lot of friends, they don't confide in very many of them. They are the most monogamous of all the birth orders. George Burns and Bob Hope are middle children. Note the longevity of their Hollywood marriages!

   This tendency to not confide in people carries over to not seeking the help of counselors, psychologists, or ministers. Second borns are usually the last ones to come to see me. First borns and only children are first because they "want to get things fixed." The last-born babies come for help because they're used to being cared for and given advice. But the middle borns have developed a mental toughness and independence that comes from being squeezed at both ends as they grew up. They prefer to "tough it out alone" and smooth the oceans of life for themselves.

4. *Statistics show middle borns are often the best bets to stay married.*[3] This is probably a natural reaction to growing up in homes where they didn't feel important or

even welcome. They want to make their marriages work and they will hang in there with unfaithful, abusive, dominating, or controlling spouses to the bitter end.

The Case of the "Peace Pipe Pleaser"

But even middle borns have their limits. I recently counseled Marianne, a middle-born, superpleasing wife, and her only-child, controlling husband, Henry, who was an orthopedic surgeon. They had been married twenty-three years, and for the past five years Marianne had been writing bitter notes and thoughts about her husband, who was in a doctor's typical syndrome: overworked, overscheduled, and seldom home.

Marianne had managed to smooth things over for eighteen years, but then it all started to go sour. That's when she started writing the notes, which she never sent but simply kept in a drawer. Writing the notes was a way to cope with her frustration. She was tired of having to continually make peace in her family, which included two teenagers. When she tried to talk about it with her husband, all she got was a grunt or, "I know you can take care of it." This couple, by the way, flew in to see me from a quite distant city. This is common for pleaser personalities who don't want anyone to know they have problems and that life is not perfect.

And what did Marianne put in her angry notes? She poured out her rage at how "everyone always wanted a piece of her." She had to handle everything at home and keep the two boys happy. In fact, with her husband off busy with his career, she turned into something of an indulgent mother who was willing to make peace at any price. The result was that she had two boys who were anything but pleasers. They dominated Mom and responded to all her permissiveness and indulgence by treating her like dirt.

Finally, Marianne had enough and came to see me. Somehow she got hubby to come along, and we sorted it out. Our first major step toward healing the marriage was her burning of all the poison-pen notes she had written her husband for the last five years. In addition, she burned all of her self-help books—the ones that tell you how to be a complete and fulfilled woman and have it all with almost no effort.

What happened was quite simple, really. (When counseling goes right, everything seems simple.) I told Marianne that if she wanted to make any real progress or find a balance in life, she had to forget the option to break up her marriage to try to "get rid of the problem." She would still have the boys to contend with. And while her husband drove her crazy, she admitted that she still loved him a great deal.

So Marianne made the commitment and said, "This is my marriage. I'm not going anywhere. I really do love Henry and I'm going to start to be positive. I'm going to start looking at his good qualities."

And so after one or two counseling sessions, she went to Henry and said, "Henry, you're really a nice man. You are loyal, hardworking, and you value your family. I really appreciate the things you do for us."

Did Henry growl and tell her to get lost? Not on your peace pipe! His chest puffed out like a pigeon's, and the first thing he asked me the next time they came in was, "What did you talk to my wife about?"

"I have no magic dust," I told him. "This is something she decided."

As Marianne continued making a positive approach to her husband, she made all kinds of discoveries. A pleaser to the core, she had always asked him, "What's wrong?"

"Nothing's wrong!" he would snap.

"Well, do you want me to get this or do you want me to do that?" she would say.

"No, just leave me alone," Henry would bark.

The simple truth was, Henry wanted more physical expression of love—in a word, sex. But instead of telling Marianne, he would give her the silent treatment and try to lose himself in work.

I asked Henry what he would prefer his wife do when he got the "long jaws" and started to go into his shell.

He said, "If she'd just come over and touch me, it would be okay."

"But I've tried that and you've pushed me away," Marianne protested.

Henry got a little red in the face and admitted that this was his typical, immature reaction. As I said earlier, once the grain is in the wood, you don't change it. But what you can change is behavior. Marianne started to persist and brought Henry out of his shell.

Once out of that shell, Henry started taking a more active part in helping with the boys, who by now were in their mid-teens. One of them was still too young to have a driver's license, so he wanted to get a dirt bike.

In the past, Marianne would probably have given in because her son would get upset and start to demonstrate his own version of "long jaws" mixed with loud complaints about not being loved.

Over the years, whenever there was any kind of squeak in the family machine, Marianne's immediate reaction was to whip out her peace pipe and her oil can filled with appeasement. Actually, her husband really had more sense in areas of Reality Discipline for children than she did. One of the positive results of our counseling was that Marianne started deferring to her husband about how to handle the boys.

Henry told the son who wanted a dirt bike, "No, I'm sorry, we aren't doing that." In the past the boy had always waited for Mom to come to his rescue. But now she began backing off and letting Henry have more to say about the parenting. And, of course, Henry responded as any only child would, with a decisive "let's do things right" approach.

The two teenagers weren't too happy at first, but once they saw they couldn't play Mom against Dad any longer, they settled down and decided to live with it. The result is that the whole family is happier and Marianne, the pleaser, is learning that her controlling husband can do some pleasing of his own.

Tips for Middle-Born Pleasers

1. *Realize that your strength is probably your weakness.* You've grown up learning how to negotiate, mediate, and keep things smoothed over. You may be like Mabel—a "peace pipe pleaser" who was willing to avoid trouble at just about any price. You don't want to turn into Wilma, the female wrestler, but you do want to stop being Wanda Wimp. Use your negotiating skills to do more confronting and less appeasing.

2. *Realize that keeping the oceans of life smooth can be a real trap.* I mentioned in this chapter the irony of the second-born pleaser who might be very social and have a lot of friends but isn't very good at communicating at a deeper

level. Under that quiet surface, all kinds of storms can be brewing because you are not communicating.

If it's difficult for you to express yourself verbally at a deep or intense level, try writing your spouse notes—positive, loving ones, of course, not the kind that Marianne wrote to Henry but never sent.

I recall counseling two middle-born pleasers who were having trouble communicating in marriage. The wife started writing hubby little positive notes and tucking them in his suitcase when he took trips. She also sent him cards more often than just Christmas and birthdays. This simple effort to communicate at a new and deeper level left her feeling far less trapped as mother of their two small children, and left the husband far more eager to come home and say, "What can I do to help?"

I know some of these solutions sound terribly simplistic, but the truth is, solutions to problems *are* simple. What is difficult is putting them into action. Even if something seems crazy and absolutely "not for you," try it anyway at least once. You may be surprised at the results.

A Last Born's Pleasing Ways May Be Manipulative

The last-born babies of the family usually try to please for much different reasons than their older brothers and sisters. The little last born looks up and sees people above him who are bigger, faster, stronger, and quicker with the tongue. That's why the baby of the family often becomes manipulative, charming, a show-off—the comedian who's always good for a laugh.

It isn't that last borns all read Bill Cosby's biography and decide they want to become comedians. The little clowns actually want to be taken seriously, but the only way they can get the world to pay attention to them is to make people laugh and smile.

I'm a classic illustration of that very fact. At age eight, while trying to lead a cheer for my sister's high school basketball team (I was "mascot"), I got it all wrong and the place literally dissolved into gales of laughter. Was I embarrassed? At age eight, I thought it was great! I decided that would be my mission in life—to make people laugh, to have them pay attention to my outrageous behavior.

Besides, I really didn't have a whole lot more than that going for me—or at least so I thought. My older sister, Sally, was a first-born, straight A, perfect 10 person. To this day, you move through her house on a clear vinyl runner over a light-blue carpet. And the Lord have mercy on your soul if you wander off that runner with muddy feet!

My older brother, Jack, was a good, solid middle child who was a B+ student, captain of the high school football team, and had a lot of friends—except for me. Jack's favorite pastime was trying to lose me in the woods when I tried to tag along with him and his buddies.

With all that firepower above me, it just didn't seem as if anything worked. Schoolwork was no fun because I couldn't possibly match Sally and Jack. Do you remember the system some teachers used for rating the reading groups at school? There were the Bluebirds, who could read very well, the Redbirds, who weren't bad, and then there were the Crows. In reading group, I was Kevin the Crow, but at home I picked up the nickname "Cub," which has stuck with me to this day. Cubs are cute, they make people laugh and smile, and that is still my favorite sport in life. I love counseling and helping people get their families back on an even keel. But what really turns me on is to get in front of

an audience and share stories, anecdotes, and illustrations that make them laugh as well as learn.

So where does the pleaser come in if you're a last-born baby of the family? Last-born little girls are usually treated as "Baby Princess." They don't go around saying, "I'll show them!" as much as they say, "I'll let them show me how much they love me." The last-born female often becomes "Daddy's little girl," and if she has a good relationship with him, one where Daddy is present and loving without being too indulgent or permissive, she learns to please men with her charming ways.

Alfred Adler observes that many youngest children desire to excel but lack self-confidence because their older brothers and sisters always seem so much stronger and more capable. Adler believes that these "defeated" younger children frequently shy away from tasks and make excuses for not meeting responsibilities. This copping out doesn't necessarily suggest a lack of ambition as much as a different type of ambition that is expressed by wiggling out of situations and problems in order to "avoid the danger of an actual test of ability, so far as possible."[4]

I don't see a lot of last-born wives in my counseling practice, but when one does come in, it is usually because her charm doesn't work on the controller she married. I constantly emphasize that no personality system is foolproof and works the same every time for every couple. As many a woman can tell you, he was a shining knight and a totally responsive, loving, charming fellow—until the sound of the wedding bells died away. Sometimes it comes out on the honeymoon; often it comes out in the first few months of marriage. Prince Charming is really a controller in disguise, and he makes life miserable for Daddy's little girl, who's always been able to please—until now.

Baby Princess Pairs Off with the Dentist

I think of Nancy, a last born who was the only girl in a family of four children. After three boys, you can imagine how Mom and Dad treated little Nancy. She wasn't just Baby Princess, she was Queen of the Realm. Even her brothers worshiped her and treated her with kindness and affection. And so Nancy married Bruce, a first-born dentist who made all the right moves and said all the right things during their courtship.

Because Nancy had always been treated so well, she had grown up to be very confident on the outside. She seemed to be able to handle situations with grace, sophistication, and good common sense. But as colicky children started to arrive, and sleepless night followed sleepless night for both of them, Bruce's explosive temper bubbled to the surface.

In my years of counseling, some of the more exacting types of first borns I have seen are those who choose a profession such as dentistry or surgery. They are always on a tight schedule, under intense pressure, and want their world to be orderly, carefully orchestrated, and never chaotic.

For Nancy, life soon turned into one big trip to the dentist. When Bruce got home from a hard day of drilling, filling, and scraping, he was in no mood for shrill giggles and arguments between his two little girls. Nancy and her daughters soon learned to "walk on eggs" around Daddy, and that's what finally brought Nancy to me.

Fortunately, while Bruce had a short fuse, he was a long way from being a woman-hating misogynist. We finally got him to come in to see me, and taking an initial session to win his confidence, I opened our second interview by asking, "Bruce, when I talked to Nancy last week, she mentioned that there are times when you really blow your cool. I imagine there are many precipitating factors that trigger the temper outbursts. Would you mind sharing your own insights on this? I'd love to hear your side of it."

Bruce admitted that this was the way he had controlled people all his life, from his permissive mother to his teachers and friends. His father had run away with another woman when he was very small, and Bruce had never related well to the man his mother picked for remarriage. His stepfather "just stayed out of it" when Bruce threw his temper tantrums, and he grew up learning that this was how he could get people to do what he wanted them to do—just show them some power, some anger. They usually backed off and gave him what he wanted rather than take a stand.

I got Bruce to see that he was using his temper to keep Nancy and the girls over the proverbial barrel and make them knuckle under. He had a basic need to control Nancy, and what better way to control a pleasing "Daddy's little girl" than with a temper.

Bruce also recognized that he used criticism with precision and accuracy. He was very good at blaming Nancy for any inadequacy or imperfection he found when he got home from his day with the drill. They began to make progress in improving the family relationship when Bruce started making a real effort to quit using his temper as a weapon, and Nancy and the girls were able to stop walking on eggs and start relating to him as the loving husband and father he really wanted to be.

What also helped Bruce was learning that in his work as a dentist he had a tendency to accumulate a great deal of tension—and anger. He needed to "let off steam," all right, but not by venting it on his family. In recent years, some psychologists have made it sound healthy to vent and just "let all that anger go." In too many cases, however, this just gives a person an excuse to dump all over other people, especially family members. "It's much better," I told Bruce, "to share with Nancy and tell her when you've had a tough day and feel tense and frustrated. But the key is to always communicate with her instead of trying to control her with anger."

Tips for Last-Born Pleasers

1. *If your marriage has turned out to be something far less than you expected, examine your motives for your pleasing behavior.* Are you trying to manipulate your husband or simply get his attention?

Check your personal habits and see if they are offsetting your pleasing, coy ways. For example, many last borns are messies. If you're married to a first-born perfectionist, your basic problem may be the way the house looks when he gets home.

And if you happen to have married a last born, look out! Some of the biggest problems I see in my counseling are couples who are from the same birth order. Only children and first borns have the most trouble, followed by middle children, but last borns can clash, too. Suppose, for example, your husband is also a messy. Who is going to straighten the place up?

I am a messy last born myself, but I was fortunate enough to marry a meticulous first born who learned how to help me grow up. In our first years of marriage, I used to leave piles of my clothes all over the apartment. Sande finally got tired of it and started letting the piles mount. The day came when I couldn't get the bedroom door open, and that's when she informed me that she was my wife, not my mother. I do much better now at picking up after myself, but admittedly, Sande is the cleany in our home and I am the messy.

2. *Another area where two last borns can get into all kinds of trouble is finances.* The courtship of two last borns is often a "go for broke" good time and then, after the wedding bells, the happy couple tends to let the good times keep right on rolling.

With credit cards as available as they are, two last borns can get into financial chaos in a hurry. I can recall one couple—both babies of their families—who came to see me about their "marital tensions." In the first interview I discovered that they weren't as upset with each other as they were with the bill collectors who were hounding them day and night. Once we got them in the hands of a financial adviser, their marital tensions cleared up in a hurry.

3. *If you're a last-born wife who sees herself as a pleaser, check your motives.* While last borns are often people persons, they also struggle inside with self-centeredness. If you have natural gifts to be funny, charming, and persuasive, be sure you're trying to please your husband and the rest of your family. Ask yourself, "Am I a pleaser because I'm a carrot seeker who always wants a pat on the head? Do I try to please people because I am interested in what's in it for them, or am I really interested in *what's in it for me?*"

Beware, too, of a love for the limelight. Last borns may misinterpret a hogging of center stage for being pleasing and entertaining. Perhaps what you think is pleasing behavior is really boorish and irritating to others. Concentrate on letting other people take center stage and being interested in their feelings and ideas.

Birth Order Is Only Part of the Picture

Let me reemphasize that knowing your birth order is only part of your personality picture. It can give you important clues on how your child of the past developed her particular quirks and why you have the relationships you now enjoy or endure.

Alfred Adler believes birth order is at least as important as heredity, possibly more so. Your special position in your family, says Adler, has shaped and colored the instincts, growth patterns, and abilities with which you were born.[5]

I've taken this chapter, as well as chapter 2, to give you a short course in personality and temperament development, because I believe this information is critical to understanding what makes a pleaser tick. To sum up, here are some key points to remember:

1. *You are who you are.* No amount of reading, counseling, or studying will change the basic "grain of your wood." What you can change, however, is your behavior and your perception of yourself and those around you.

2. *The little girl you once were you still are.* You carry around this child of the past in your memory bank, and she is always making her presence felt with demands, complaints, and opinions. Does your inner child remember being Baby Princess? Perhaps your child of the past remembers being the first born who had to take care of the baby in the family as well as all the rest and felt she was dumped on most of the time. Whatever your inner child brings up, don't ever try to squelch the little girl inside; accept her, give her

her due, but don't let her run the show. Parent your little girl just as you parent your children.

3. *The relationship between a daughter and her father is crucial.* I believe it has lifelong effects and repercussions. Daughters who have negative experiences with Daddy because he is distant and unaffectionate, or because he leaves through death, divorce, or desertion, will find themselves drawn to the very same kind of man when they are ready for marriage. Again and again I hear women in my office say, "I swore I would never marry someone like my father, and here I am in exactly the kind of marriage I didn't want. Why? What is wrong with me?"

Nothing is "wrong" with this kind of woman. She needs to understand that being a patient pleaser who simply accepts being kicked in the teeth day after day is not the answer. There is much you can do about being an abused and disrespected pleaser in a controlling world, and the next two sections of this book will tell you what and how. In the following chapters we will examine major myths and lies that keep pleasers trapped and victimized, afraid to risk making a change, and all too willing to accept the martyr's or victim's role because "it seems to be what I deserve."

You deserve a lot more out of life than that, and I hope to tell you how to get it by exploding the myths pleasers like to believe because they are "comfortable and safe." Strangely enough, many women choose the comfortable and safe even though it is, in truth, painful and dangerous. They tell themselves:

"Everybody has to like me."
"I don't deserve much—I'm lucky it isn't worse."
"I'm sorry—it's all my fault."

"If I just try harder, everything will be okay."

"I shoulda ... I oughta ... but I'll just play it safe."

Do any of these lines sound familiar? Let's take a look at them and find out why.

PART 2

Why Pleasers Can't Say No

If there is a "common denominator" for all pleasers, it is the inability to say no to a world that seems to keep them on the defensive, feeling pressured and controlled. The next three chapters cover major problems for most pleasers: low self-esteem, guilt, and perfectionism. When a pleaser battles any one—or all three—of these enemies, she is fair game for the controllers who know just how to manipulate her, take advantage of her, or intimidate her. Fortunately, there is a lot the pleaser can do to fight back and live a more positive life. In this next section you will learn

- why pleasers want everyone to like them
- how a pleaser's stock can go up with a controller—if she is willing to make a stand
- how we teach children—especially little girls—to never say no
- how "cognitive self-discipline" can put you on the road to a higher self-image and stronger self-esteem
- why self-image is basically a matter of faith
- how to use positive self-talk to move from no power to NO! Power
- how pleasers become experts at gathering guilt
- what to expect from a controller when you try to change
- why perfectionism sets you up for failure every time
- the difference between perfectionism and seeking excellence
- how to become a "practical perfectionist" who enjoys life

4

Pleasers Battle
a Low Self-Image

"I want everybody to like me . . ."

At forty-one Sally looked older—and weary. Her big blue eyes were red and her brown hair was pulled straight back in a no-nonsense bun that said, "I haven't got time to fuss."

"I just don't seem to be able to say no," Sally admitted as she reached for a tissue. "Why do I do it? I let people use me until it's ridiculous. My neighbor Pam walks all over me. She borrows food and never pays me back. She asks me to baby-sit for her while she runs to the store, and then she stays twice as long as she said she would. Not only that, but she borrows my car to go! I know this will be hard to believe, but it's true. Just today I knew I had this appointment, but I loaned Pam my car anyway and had to take the bus to get here—with three transfers!"

"How often does Pam use your car?" I asked. "Does she ever give you any advance notice when she needs it?"

"Well, she and her husband have only one car, and he drives that to work. She has been borrowing mine since they moved next door six months ago. Some weeks it's two or three times . . . sometimes she'll call the night before, but this morning she saw a special sale in the paper and wanted to get there fast. How could I say no?"

"Very easily, if you weren't such a pleaser," I answered. "You've been in to see me several times now, and there is a definite pattern. You just don't want to risk offending Pam—or anybody else. You have a little recording going inside that keeps telling you, 'I only count when I make people happy, and if I say no they won't like me and I'll be a big zero.'"

Sally pondered my words for a few moments and then said, "Well, I don't know about the zero part, but maybe what you're saying helps explain why in high school I would take notes for my friends while they ditched class. I can remember writing a lot of their book reports and papers, just so I'd be one of the 'in group.'"

"And I suppose you worked hard to keep your boy-friends?"

Sally looked at me hard. "Why yes, as a matter of fact, I went steady with a guy in my junior and senior years and I let him go too far more than once just so he wouldn't dump me. I didn't get pregnant, but I know lots of girls who did doing that kind of stuff."

"Sally, from what you're telling me today and in the other sessions we've had, you show classic signs of being a pleaser. That is, you just can't say no. You let people walk all over you just to be liked and accepted. Fortunately, there is a lot you can do about your problem."

"Like what?" she wondered.

"First, we'll do a little exercise I use with all my clients. Usually I do it in an earlier session, but I didn't think you were ready before now. It's called a 'mini life-style quiz,' and it's based on the premise that each of us is a product of the environment that we grew up in and that we live in now. We learn to be who we are from those who surround us and live with us. So, I'd like to have you start with your family. To get started, simply give me a description of either your mother or your father. Just pick one. . . ."

All Sally's Father Had to Do Was Give Her That Look

The mini life-style workup I did on Sally is based on some principles laid down by Alfred Adler, pioneer in individual psychology, who believed that a person's *goals* are absolutely primary in understanding that person's behavior. Adler theorized that all of us follow an individual "life line" or path toward certain goals and that we really would not know what to do with ourselves were we "not oriented toward some goal."[1]

In developing my own approach to Adlerian psychology, I began tracing each client's life line in order to determine her or his life-style or style of living. Today's popular definition of the word *life-style* is not too far from what I am after when I give a mini life-style quiz to a client. I want to find out how and why a person lives and acts a certain way. A big part of the answer to that question lies in the person's goals—what the person does to obtain satisfaction and fulfillment—"happiness."

Alfred Adler said, "We cannot think, feel, will or act without the perception of some goal."[2] Where we get our individual goals depends on who and what has left an imprint on us. Not surprisingly, we usually have to go back to childhood to find out, and that is why I asked Sally to describe either her father or her mother. Let's continue with her mini life-style quiz, and to help you better understand how it works, I'll make some observations in italics as we go along.

By asking Sally to pick her father or mother, I wanted her to make an immediate judgment on which one was more influential in her life.

"I guess I'll talk about my father," she said. "Do you want his physical description or personality characteristics?"

I noted immediately that Sally was very concerned about pleasing me, even though she was doing her own life-style quiz. She was really asking, "What is the right way to do this? I want to please you—I want to do this right."

"Just describe your father—any way you wish."

"Well, he was very strict. You can bet we knew right from wrong. And we always paid attention to whatever he said. In fact, he didn't have to lay a hand on us. I never got a spanking in my entire life. All my father had to do was look at me and I snapped to. . . ."

I noticed she was using the pronoun we, *which I learned included her two younger sisters. She was the first born.*

"Tell me more about your father. What did he do for a living?"

"My dad was an engineer. He worked on a lot of highway projects," Sally continued. "He was *very* exacting and particular. He really expected a lot from himself and from all of us."

"Did he criticize you much?"

"No, not really, but he was extremely strict and sort of distant. We all knew we had to really live up to his standards or we would be in big trouble."

Whenever I give a client a mini life-style quiz, I listen for adjectives such as very *and* really. *I pay attention to what the client emphasizes, the people or experiences who are most important. Note also that her father was a very exacting man, probably a perfectionist. She had grown up having to meet his high standards at every point in life.*

"Tell me about other people in your family," I suggested.

"Mom really loved us and sacrificed a lot for us. She was always the real parent to us—easygoing—really a good mom. She never had any major hassles with anybody and always gave in to Dad and tried to make him happy."

And so we learn that Sally's mother was not the major psychological force in her life. In fact, the mother had been a role model who taught Sally how to be passive in the presence of a controlling, authoritarian husband.

"Describe yourself as a little girl—between the ages of, say, five and twelve. What do you remember about yourself?"

"Well, I was always pretty cautious. I always tried to do what I was told. I loved school and almost always got good grades. I never really gave my parents any trouble—I guess I was practically a Miss Goody Two Shoes. I remember once, though, I did lie to my mom about some change that mysteriously disappeared from her purse. But I never lied to my dad—never!"

Sally's pleaser pattern continued to form as she described her life as a young girl in school. She was never absent, took part in everything, always had the right answers, but was never pushy or controlling—the kind of pupil teachers love to have around to remind them that they aren't working in a zoo.

"In kindergarten I got the lead part for a play that we did for all the mothers," Sally recalled. "The teacher was always picking me out for things like that."

"Tell me more about the time you lied to your mother," I prompted.

"Well, actually it was my sisters who took the money, but I sort of took the blame because I didn't want them to get in trouble," Sally said. "I never would have stolen anything from my mother's purse myself. I didn't have the nerve. I was always worried about doing what's right and telling the truth. But Mom knew I lied the minute I said that I'd taken the money. So she punished all of us. It was one of the few times she ever did that."

As her mini life-style workup continued, Sally shared quite a bit more from her growing-up years, and a great deal of it pinpointed quite clearly how she had become a pleaser. One incident that she recalled about a certain Father's Day stood out. . . .

"I remember when I was about eight or nine and I made breakfast in bed for my mom and dad on Father's Day. I didn't really do a very good job. I think I burned the bacon and the eggs were runny, but Mom and Dad said it was wonderful. When I got to thinking about it several years later, I realized that they really didn't eat much of the breakfast and they were just being nice to tell me it was so good."

Sally's recollections fit perfectly with the characteristics of the first-born child, who is often much more vulnerable to criticism and is driven by a desire to be perfect in the eyes of her parents, teachers, and other authority figures. The first born often takes everything on her shoulders. For example, by covering for her sisters, Sally became the "ice cutter on the lake of life." Or, to put it in football terms, she often chose to carry the ball and block for her sisters at the same time. Later in the mini life-style discussion, we jumped from her childhood up to the present. . . .

"Sally, we've looked at your childhood and now we want to talk about what you're doing as an adult besides putting up with Pam. I believe you work part-time. . . ."

Pam Wasn't Sally's Real Problem

Sally took a deep breath and launched into a description of her life at present. As is often the case, everything she had told me up to that point had simply been a test to see what kind of a person I was. Could I be trusted? She did have a problem with her neighbor Pam, but Pam was not her real problem. The one who was really taking advantage of her pleasing nature was her husband, Tom.

"I guess some people would call me the typical super-mom," Sally said with a wry smile. "People are always asking me how I do it. I just tell them I don't think much about it. I just try to keep everything going smoothly for the family, but it's getting to me. Actually, I guess I try to keep everything smooth for everybody I know. And I'm getting tired—in fact, I think I'm a mess."

In the next thirty minutes I learned that Sally had always pitched in and worked off and on during the fourteen years she and Tom had been married. They had three children, ages eleven, eight, and five, and Tom had his own business, installing ceramic tile. Besides working part-time as a hairdresser, Sally did Tom's books as well as keeping her home spotless, the kids well fed and well dressed, and managing the checking account for the family.

"How do you and Tom get along? How would you rate your marriage relationship?"

"Not too bad, I guess. The one thing that has really been hard is that he is so tight with money. I have to watch every penny I spend for family things, and of course, I've got to keep the books for his business in perfect order. But I guess it could be worse . . . I'm lucky to have a good provider like Tom. . . ."

It was becoming very evident that Sally was like many pleasers. Her self-esteem, which had never been very high, was shaky at best.

"Tell me a little bit more about how you have to handle the money," I quizzed her.

After a little more sparring, what was really eating Sally came flooding out. She always had to beg for dollars, whether it was for taking a friend to lunch or buying a pair of shoes. Whatever the expenditure, she had to ask Tom's permission. She would say, "Honey, there's plenty of money in the checking account and I need to write a check for a new pair of shoes." Tom's stock answer was, "No, there isn't any money in the account. Do you think money grows on trees?"

"This has been going on since we were married," Sally said heatedly. "Sometimes he switches his strategy and gives me permission to spend some money. Then later he takes cheap shots about how much everything costs—as if I am a lousy shopper or too extravagant—but we really are doing well financially. Just yesterday I learned that Tom had contacted the bank without my knowledge and arranged for a reserve credit line on our checking account of ten thousand dollars. And I've had to beg to write a check for a pair of twenty-eight-dollar shoes! I can't even get our washer fixed. I've been lugging the laundry down to the Laundromat for the last month because Tom says we don't have any money!"

"What you're telling me, Sally, is that in effect Tom has arranged for a ten-thousand-dollar cushion at the bank in the unlikely event of a bounced check, but he didn't want you to know that. He wanted you to think you had to watch every penny for fear a check might bounce."

"You have the picture. And just in case you're wondering where I got the money to pay for my counseling, I'm putting it on the VISA card and hoping Tom won't find out."

"Sally, I'm afraid that what we have here is the classic match-up of the pleaser and the controller. You've grown up learning to please. Remember when I asked you to describe either your mother or father for me? You chose your father first, and it's obvious from your descriptions of your parents that he was by far the more significant person in your life. You really toed the mark for him, although he never gave you much attention or affection. And your mom was a role model who showed you how to be a pleaser to a controlling husband."

As we probed into Sally's life and learned how she and Tom functioned, all of a sudden it hit her. . . .

"You know, I really can't believe it, but as we're talking right now it's becoming clear that Tom is a great deal like my father. I never thought about it much until now. . . ."

"Sally, it's no mystery that you grew up and found a man just like your dad. Most of the women I counsel marry men who are like their fathers in one way or another—especially when the fathers are controllers. Tom is like a lot of men. He wants to control you and he does it with money, which is very typical."

Sally just sat and looked at me, not saying anything. But the light was beginning to dawn. I continued. . . .

"Sally, your neighbor Pam is not your real problem. Your real problem is Tom and his control over you, particularly with money. It's my guess it took you a long time to decide to come in to see me, and you're ready to do something to change things."

"You're right about that . . . I just got thinking, *Here you are, in your early forties, and you still get jerked around like a little kid. . . .*"

"I often tell my clients that they can't change who they really are. That little girl who tried to please teachers and parents back there in your childhood is still with you. The grain of your wood is set, but the good news, from a therapeutic standpoint, is that because you've learned to be this way, you can also learn to act differently. You can change your behavior. You don't have to be a hostage to your old habits."

"So what do you think I should do?" Sally wanted to know.

"Use action instead of words. Call the repairman and have him come and fix the washer. Don't tell Tom you're doing it, just have it done while he's at work and he'll see the bill soon enough."

"But he'll be very angry," Sally protested. "He'll fuss and fume and carry on. I don't think it's worth it. . . ."

"Oh, yes, it is," I said. "Tom has banked on your inability to confront him and stand up for yourself for years. You've gotten fed up or you wouldn't have come to see me. Now is the time to make a stand in this simple way. I think you should do it, before things get worse and you get angry enough to do something serious."

Sally Said She'd "Try to Change," But . . .

Sally left, muttering that I was probably breaking up her marriage but she would try it. I didn't like the sound of that phrase *try it*. That tells me people wish they could change but they don't necessarily have the conviction.

My hunch was correct. The next week Sally canceled her appointment and I did not hear from her for another four weeks. Finally she called and arranged to come in the following Wednesday.

"I finally worked up enough nerve to face you," she told me. "I just couldn't do it. I even made the appointment with the repairman, but I chickened out at the last minute and canceled him. I'm just too afraid of what Tom will say or do."

"Sally, you don't have to apologize to me, because you really don't answer to me for anything. I'm simply a counselor who is trying to help you make some important decisions, but only you can do the deciding. All I can tell you is that without action on your part, you'll just spin your wheels and continue to be frustrated."

My entire session with Sally that day was more or less in the form of a "pep talk" to help her make a decisive move toward becoming a Positive Pleaser instead of an Exhausted, almost Depressed one. As she got up to leave, her big blue eyes stared right into mine and she said, "This time, I'm going to *do it*."

I looked forward to Sally's next appointment with a great deal of curiosity. I never did worry too much about how Tom would react. Oh, no doubt he would huff and puff a bit, but it wouldn't go much further than that. The way Sally had described Tom told me he was a typical controller but not really abusive or mean.

It turned out I was right. Sally couldn't wait to tell me what happened.

"I got the washer fixed, just as you suggested," she explained. "Tom was really angry, but I could see that a lot of it was bluff. He wanted me to get back to my 'Yes Tom, of course, Tom' behavior that he was so familiar with. I simply told him I couldn't keep working, taking care of the house, and hauling laundry out to the Laundromat, too. I also let him know I knew about the ten-thousand-dollar credit line at the bank."

"Double congratulations!" I told her. "You've taken a big step in the right direction. Just about everybody in your life has kept you off balance and walking on eggs. Now you've finally gotten just a little taste of how it feels to please yourself for a change."

"Well, it did feel good, I guess, but now I've got some different problems. Once Tom saw he couldn't get anywhere by getting all upset, he went into sort of a deep freeze. We don't talk much right now. And when my mother came for the weekend, Tom went out of his way to put me in my place a few times. He made it a point to say that *his* mother took the laundry to the Laundromat for years. . . ."

"Good for his mother," I responded. "But he's not married to his mother. He's married to you, and you want a little more respect and some better treatment. Stick to your guns."

Sally spent an additional two months in counseling, quite a bit longer than my average client, because I make it a point to do short-term therapy that helps people take action and change behavior as quickly as possible. But Sally was so trapped in a life-style of pleasing that she needed the extra encouragement and support. In addition, she had to buck strong resistance from Tom, who, like any typical controller, didn't like his wife's new behavior. I told her that when a pleasing wife starts to stand up for her rights, even a little bit, she can count on a controlling husband's getting worse—at least temporarily. But I assured her that if she hung in there, things would improve.

To some people, it may sound as if Sally had problems serious enough to put her down at the bottom of the Pyramid of Pleasers discussed in chapter 1. But compared to many women I've counseled, Sally was a long way from a Supersuffering Pleaser. I placed her somewhere between Played-Out and Depressed. It wouldn't have been too long, however, until she could have wound up at the very bottom of the pile, where she would have been really suffering.

My goal was to help Sally climb toward the Positive level and remain a very pleasing person, but at the same time gain the respect and decent treatment she wanted and certainly deserved, particularly from her family.

As the weeks went by, Sally took tiny but definite steps of improvement. Actually, her new behavior had gotten through to Tom more than she suspected. When she got that washer fixed, Tom did make all kinds of protests, but nonetheless her stock went up as far as his respect was concerned. He wouldn't admit it, of course, and a lot of his comments and carping were designed to keep Sally thinking that he was as much "in charge" as ever.

And of course, on Sally's side, one act of boldness led to others. For example, she took an afternoon off and invited a friend to lunch—on her. When Tom asked her where she had been, she told him and he said nothing.

I could almost watch Sally's self-esteem rise by the week. All her life she had been told she couldn't say no, that the only word she could say to anyone was yes, and that she could never make waves, while everybody else did what he or she pleased. Now she was finding out that she could say no to other people and yes to herself without feeling guilty.

And Whatever Happened to Presumptuous Pam?

And what about Pam, the neighbor with no wheels who always used Sally's? Not long after Sally stood up to Tom and got her washer fixed, Pam called again and wanted to use the car:

"Sally, I'm sorry to ask on such short notice, but I really need to borrow your car to run over to my mother's. She just called and wants me to see her new couch. It was delivered today."

Sally took a deep breath and said, "Pam, I'm going to need my car most of today. Why don't you call your mother and see if she can come pick you up. Or, you could take a bus. I did one day when you borrowed my car and I had to go to the doctor."

Pam huffed and puffed just a little and let Sally know that this was going to be a "real problem" but she understood.

About a week later, Pam tried again. As usual, she gave no notice to speak of—she needed to borrow the car to run to the grocery store. "Pam, I wonder if you would want to wait until after lunch," Sally suggested. "I'll be going to the store myself and we can go together."

"But why can't I use it now?" Pam wanted to know. "It won't be as convenient to go after lunch."

"No, Pam, I may need the car this morning. I would rather not loan my car to you except for real emergencies. I'll be glad to take you with me this afternoon, but that's the best I can do."

Very soon after, Sally noticed a late-model compact car sitting in Pam's driveway. It turned out to be the second car her husband had been planning on buying but simply "hadn't gotten around to it."

When Sally started using gentle assertiveness with Pam, I knew she was well on her way to becoming a Positive Pleaser. She would probably always struggle with Tom and his hang-ups about money, but she had acquired a new balance of power in her marriage and had actually grown in stature in her husband's eyes. The day Sally left counseling she was headed for a department store to buy a new outfit for Easter. "It's a surprise for Tom," she said with a wink. "I'm sure he'll like it!"

Why Is It So Hard to Say No?

Many of my female clients are a lot like Sally. They wonder why they find it so hard to say no. Across the nation all kinds of classes are held on assertiveness training, especially for women. Books such as *Don't Say Yes When You Want to Say No*[3] and *How to Be an Assertive (Not Aggressive) Woman in Life, in Love, and on the Job*[4] are best sellers.

I suppose all kinds of complicated reasons can be found that some people—especially many women—can't say no, or at least they can't say it very easily. My experience tells me one cause is the way women are trained while growing up. Their parents, other members of the family, and other authority figures often teach children that *no* is practically a four-letter word. I know many parents (my wife and I included) who have said to their children at one time or another: "What do you mean, *no*? Don't you *dare* say no to me!"

A much better response to a child who stamps her little foot and says, "No!" to coming in from play is, "Honey, I know you're having a good time, but you have to come in now. We're going to be having dinner in a little while." If the child still refuses to come, pick her up and carry her inside. One bit of specific action is worth thousands of futile words, and you have not deliberately programmed your child to never say no.

The point is, there are ways to train your child with what I call Reality Discipline,[5] which helps them become responsible individuals with the healthy kind of self-esteem that enables them to be accountable for their decisions. Frankly, there are times when our children should say no—to danger, to strangers, to situations that aren't right for them. The higher their self-esteem, the better they will perform under pressure.

Self-esteem is a complicated area, and no hard-and-fast judgments can be made on why some children grow up to have a good self-image and high self-esteem while others have an extremely negative feeling about themselves. In earlier chapters we looked at some possible causes for low self-esteem. Many adults carry an inner child of the past who remembers parents who were flaw pickers, drill sergeants, or wicked stepmothers. Overcoercive parents can put out a child's candle of self-esteem faster than anybody.

Ironically, parents who are overly permissive—the wimps and the Santa Clauses—can also turn out children with low self-esteem. Why? The child thinks, *They don't care what I do, so I guess I'm not very important!*

If you feel a serious lack of self-esteem, there is no point in blaming your parents and saying to yourself, "It's my little girl from the past. The grain of my wood is set and I'll always have people walk on me. I'll never be able to say no." Instead, work on raising your self-image—your perception of who you really are and what you can do and be.

Changing a low self-image and increasing your self-esteem is not done overnight. There are thousands of books that have all kinds of useful information on self-esteem. I believe, however, that the best approach to gaining a higher self-image and stronger self-esteem is using what I call "cognitive self-discipline." Your self-image and self-esteem will not rise until you start thinking and then acting differently. *Cognitive self-discipline* is just a fancy term for using your head and thinking through why you do what you do. "To cogitate" is to think carefully, to consider intently. When a pleaser starts to use cognitive self-discipline, she will not fall into the same old pleasing patterns and behaviors without giving it a second thought. To change your behavior, you need to think twice and ask yourself, *Is this good for me? Is this right for me? What is the best way for me to behave in this situation?* When confronted with a social situation, it is wise to practice cognitive self-discipline. Ask yourself, *How would the "old me" react in this situation? How is the "new me" going to react?*

When you start changing your behavior, your attitudes, emotions, and feelings will change as well. But until you make those changes, you will continue to see yourself as

- someone who doesn't really deserve respect from anyone.
- someone who couldn't possibly have much importance.
- someone who always blows it and is at fault in every situation.

Keep telling yourself these lies and your self-image will remain on the low side of the scale, along with your feelings of self-worth.

105

Take That First Step of Faith

The first step toward higher self-esteem is to realize that your self-image shouldn't come from what other people think of you. I realize this is difficult for many women to understand (and many men, for that matter). In today's Yuppie culture, we place a great weight on what others think of us, our image, how we look. Women, in particular, are pressured to be concerned about looking youthful, chic, and "with it."

As long as you get your self-image from external sources, you will never be your real self, and you will always be at the mercy of what others want to tell you and how others want to treat you. Unfortunately, there are far more people in the world who will want to manipulate you and use you for their own particular ends than there are people who will want to build you up and encourage you.

After nearly twenty years of counseling work, I have concluded that self-image is basically a matter of faith. To have a good self-image, you must wrestle with the question of what life is all about. This takes us into the spiritual area, which I often find makes some clients very uncomfortable. They tell me, "I don't want to talk about religion."

I answer, "I don't, either. I want to talk about the spiritual part of who you are. After all, you have a physical side, an emotional side, a mental side, and a social side to your personality. But what about your spirit?"

Some of my clients are surprised to learn I believe in a Creator. I believe every human being on this planet was created by God and is here to serve His purpose. I can never get away from the thought that we even all have our own fingerprints. Perhaps this is God's way of saying, "Yes, you really are one of My children. You are unique, special, and you don't have to compare yourself with everybody else in this world. I love you just as you are."

Stop Worrying about What Other People Do

Another major step toward better self-esteem is to realize that you really can't control what other people do. You aren't accountable for what other people do. The only behavior you can change is your own.

As I work with women like Sally and all the other pleasers described in this book, I try to get them to trust in their own uniqueness. Once they commit themselves to change, they can start seeing themselves objectively. More important, they can start seeing other people more objectively and recognize the traps that controllers set for them.

Pleasers walk into these controller traps of their own free will, using their own two feet, and taking one step at a time. But pleasers can also learn to stop, assess the situation, and back out of these traps or avoid them. The key for every pleaser is to stop and think about what is happening. Is she responding in her "normal" pleasing way?

For example, when Sally was badgered about money by her husband, she always deferred and tried to get along with less or none. She probably would have hauled her laundry to the Laundromat for the rest of her life if she hadn't decided enough was enough.

She might have loaned her car to Pam for the next several years if she hadn't been able to finally say, "Things must change. I must change. I will act differently and not respond with my usual attempt to be sure people love me and like me."

When I counsel overly pleasing women, I always assure them that realizing "enough is enough" does not mean they have to abandon their warmth and consideration for others. I am of the firm opinion the world can use many more Positive Pleasers who live to please others, *but who do it for the right reasons.* The Positive Pleaser gives to others but she also receives the respect and consideration any person deserves. The Positive Pleaser does not have to settle for being tossed a few crumbs intended to keep her happy and "in line."

Pleasers Often Settle for Tidbits of Attention

A few years ago the world was shocked by the murder of Dr. Herman Tarnower, well-known developer of the "Scarsdale Diet." His killer was Jean Harris, with whom Tarnower had a close relationship for some fourteen years. Columnist Ellen Goodman accurately described Jean Harris as a woman who had "learned all too well how to swallow mouthfuls of humiliation in return for tidbits of attention." But those tidbits were never enough, and her anger finally exploded into tragedy.

Jean Harris was "grateful for small favors" until the small favors did not suffice any longer. She decided enough was *not* enough, and driven by rage, humiliation, and frustration, she took another life.

Not all pleasers go over the edge as Jean Harris did, but I have counseled many of them who swallow rage and humiliation because they believe that "something is better than nothing." They pay for this with ulcers, headaches, colitis, nervous stomachs, and any number of other ailments. To continually repress rage and humiliation is as bad as swallowing poison.

When you are "grateful for small favors," you have a serious problem with your priorities, which is caused by low self-esteem and a poor self-image. Instead of getting what you want and need (respect, love, fulfillment, and good mental and physical health, not to mention enough money to spend on yourself and your home), you will settle for disrespect, neglect, and indifference. Possibly you may be enduring real pain and suffering, if you are unfortunate enough to be hooked up with a misogynist or addictive personality (*see* chapters 9 and 10).

The pleaser with poor self-esteem plays the game of "at least I have something. . . ." Her husband can be a controller who dominates her by withholding money, as Sally's husband did. Or he can be much worse: a womanizer, a booze hound, or a loser who can't find a job and isn't looking that hard. He may be a liar, a bully, and a neglectful father as well as a neglectful husband. No matter what the pleaser has to deal with, she still tells herself, *At least I have a man. At least I don't have it as bad as Mary Ellen down the street. . . .*

No matter where the pleaser may land on the Pyramid described in chapter 1, she lets others run her life to one degree or another. At work she puts up with fellow workers who take advantage of her or bosses who load her down with extra work because they know she will do it. After all, she's grateful for small favors. She is glad she has a job.

Besides, she knows she probably couldn't get a better position. Why, she just talked to Marjorie the other day. Marjorie's been out of work for months, and she's far better qualified. She would be a fool to think she could switch jobs or get something better.

Anytime the pleaser plays the comparison game, she is in deep trouble. She has been comparing herself to others all her life and coming up short. That's why she tries to please—to make others happy. She always gives in because, after all, the other person is always right, always smarter, and how in the world could she—the pleaser—ever have an opinion or an idea that might be better? And so the pleaser is willing to settle for much less than half a loaf. She takes the small crumbs and is glad to get them.

Another game the pleaser with low self-esteem will often play is, "I'm too old," "I'm too fat," "I'm not pretty enough," "I'm not smart enough," and on and on. Again, the pleaser's self-image has her trapped behind bars of her own making. When you see yourself as too old, not pretty, not capable, you have nowhere to go. You think you must stick it out where you are and do the best you can.

Tips for Pleasers Who Want to Change

The bad news about low self-esteem and low self-image is that you don't solve these twin problems just like that. It took you years to build your own little prison of feelings of poor self-worth.

The good news is that because you built this prison yourself, you can also take it apart, bar by bar. Here are some positive steps you can begin taking immediately:

1. *Develop the spiritual side of your life.* Get on speaking terms with God and thank Him for not making any mistakes, including you. If you already have a personal relationship with God, deepen that relationship by becoming more active in a house of worship where you can be comfortable not only with the theology but with the way the other members live their lives. A judgmental, pharisaical, ultraperfectionist atmosphere is no place for a pleaser who is trying to raise her self-esteem.

2. *Use positive self-talk.* Turn off the negative tapes that keep going around inside your head. Those were probably made by that little girl of the past who is with you. Tell her

to be quiet and start talking to yourself in positive ways. The term *self-talk* is current jargon for what you say to yourself all day long, sometimes out loud and often in your thoughts. Psychologists differ on how fast we can talk to ourselves—some say four hundred to six hundred words a minute, others say thirteen hundred words a minute. Whatever the speed, start telling yourself positive things. I particularly like a passage from the New Testament in which the apostle Paul lays down the best foundation you could find anywhere for positive self-talk:

> Fix your thoughts on what is true and good and right. Think about things that are pure and lovely, and dwell on the fine, good things in others. Think about all you can praise God for and be glad about it.[6]

To that I would add only, "Dwell on the fine, good things in *yourself.*" Turn off the old self-talk that reminds you that you don't measure up, you aren't worth liking for yourself, and you have to work at keeping everybody happy so they will like you. Instead of the old lies, tell yourself some new and refreshing truths:

"God made me and loves me as much as anyone else on the planet."

"What I think is important, too."

"I don't have to be perfect . . . I just have to be me!"

"If I want respect, I have to act as if I want to be respected."

"I am a good person."

"I'm a classic—one of a kind—no one on earth is *exactly* like me."

3. *Stop playing comparison games with your friends, neighbors, and others in your life.* While their feelings and rights are certainly important, what they think of you really isn't.

What you think of yourself is far more important. Start speaking up and giving your opinion. You don't have to be abrasive or obnoxious. Just be your pleasant, pleasing self, but be firm about what you really think. You'll be amazed at how much better you feel about yourself and how much more respect you start to receive.

I like what my friend Sonya Friedman, author of *Smart Cookies Don't Crumble*, says about saying no.[7] Too many women go through their lives with no power instead of NO! Power. There is nothing beneficial or admirable about living life with no power. When you have NO! Power you stand up for your rights, but you are fair and get your share of respect and consideration without depriving or hurting other people. With NO! Power, you can make changes that really matter. With NO! Power, you can get the mutual respect you have been looking for. Best of all, NO! Power will improve your marriage, your ability to be a good parent, and your other relationships.

Try it. Take one small step and it might become a giant leap toward a better life. Say yes to NO! Power now!

5

The Guilt Gatherers of Life

"I should have . . . I ought to . . . it's all my fault!"

A sure sign of low self-esteem in the pleaser is that she will take the blame for almost everything. Whether it's a business associate, a friend, or family member, the pleaser assumes responsibility for keeping the relationship going. If something goes wrong, if there is a bump or a blowup, she says, "I should have handled that better—*it's all my fault.*"

Driven by an overly sensitive conscience, the pleaser is an expert at what I call "guilt gathering." Because she has always had to play by somebody else's rules—the authority figures who have made her toe the mark—she seems to pile up one infraction after another until she is burdened with an overwhelming load of false guilt.

The pleasing guilt gatherer often lets her children do a number on her. For example, little Suzy doesn't do her homework for three nights in a row. Now her book report is due in the morning and it's 9:20 p.m.—bedtime is in ten minutes. Suzy has watched her favorite sit-coms, and now she's ready to work on her report.

"Mom, would you help me with my book report? Dad says he's too busy. . . ."

"Honey, I'm sorry, but you've been up until ten o'clock or ten-thirty the past few nights and you haven't gotten up on time. Don't you think you had better get to bed at nine-thirty for a change?"

"Dad said you'd probably make me go to bed," wails Suzy. "And now I'll flunk. You *never* help me. . . ."

And Suzy storms off to bed while Mom feels a not-so-little black cloud of guilt settling slowly around her head and shoulders. "You're a bad mother," whispers the little black cloud. "Good moms *always* help their kids."

Notice that in this instance, Mom had enough backbone to say no to Suzy and let her take responsibility for planning her time better. The best thing that could happen to Suzy might be getting a bad grade on a book report because of wasting too much time watching TV, but Mom probably doesn't think about that. She is too preoccupied with her guilt gathering. And, next week, when the situation inevitably comes up again, Mom might give in and stay up with Suzy well past everybody's bedtime, trying to finish a neglected assignment.

What Mom should do is consistently refuse to bail Suzy out of her last-minute homework predicament and let her take the consequences. In addition, Mom should call the school, talk to Suzy's teacher, and tell her what's happening. This way the teacher knows Mom is trying to use some good old-fashioned Reality Discipline on Suzy, and she can work with Mom to help Suzy become a more responsible child. At the same time, Mom works on becoming a more positive, less guilt-ridden pleaser.

The pleaser has all kinds of guilty buttons that are familiar to the people who know her best: her kids, her husband, close friends, and people she works with every day. Let me tell you about two very different women who had the same problem: letting loved ones manipulate them with guilt because they thought they had to play by certain rules that weren't their own to keep the oceans of life smooth for everyone—everyone but themselves, of course.

Meet Clarissa—the Powerful Jellyfish

At thirty-seven, Clarissa had already become manager of a local bank. Slim, with brown hair, big brown eyes, and a sweet smile, she was a picture of sophistication, class, and perfect grooming. She seemed to exude confidence and poise.

I was puzzled, however, because when Clarissa had made her appointment, she mentioned she was tired of "being taken advantage of and running scared all the time." I was curious to learn why this seemingly self-assured, powerful woman felt so walked on and afraid.

"At work I make all kinds of executive decisions all day long," she told me. "I have to pass on loans, make judgments on everything from a person's character to his or her financial potential. I've handled everything from petty personnel squabbles to a mass employee protest over working conditions. And I was the one who kept my head when we were robbed. . . ."

"It sounds as if you can handle life at the bank," I observed. "Tell me about home."

At the mention of her home life, Clarissa's confidence seemed to dissolve. Her eyes, which had held mine at a steady gaze at the start of the session, went downcast as they filled with tears.

"I turn into a jellyfish and I don't know why," she said haltingly. "My husband runs me around like a little girl. I do everything I can to please him, but he treats me as if he doesn't care."

"Can you give me some examples?" I urged. Already I was suspecting that a seemingly independent, knowledgeable, and self-sufficient person at work was really a pleaser in disguise and married to a controller who knew how to make her dance to his tune at home.

"There are all kinds of little things," she replied, "but a major incident happened just last month when I scheduled a week of vacation. I set it up well in advance, according to company policy. Jim was going to take some time off too, but a couple of days before we were to leave he started thinking about changing his mind."

"Didn't he tell you?"

"Not until the night before we were to leave. Then he told me his boss had just asked for a new report and it had to be ready the following Wednesday. So there I was, all packed and ready to go on vacation, with no husband to go with."

"And you're saying this kind of thing is not unusual?"

"Well, it isn't always something as serious as leaving me high and dry for seven days alone on vacation, but he's always coming home late and not bothering to call and let me know. He expects me to get home and get dinner ready, but he often forgets the schedule. When I mention it to him, he gets upset and I usually wind up apologizing, even though he's the one who causes the problem. He claims I forget to tell him what time we are to have dinner, or that I just don't understand how busy and under pressure he is. Come to think of it, even the vacation hassle was my problem and my fault because I had forgotten to remind him of the dates. What really happened was that he never made firm plans to go, and when his boss requested the extra report, he had no prior vacation arrangement to refer back to."

As Clarissa continued, the pattern emerged. When I did a mini life-style workup on her, it was no surprise that she described her father first. She had tried so very hard, even as a little girl, to please her father, but all he ever had for her was a critical word. He was always the one who told her she should have done it this way or that way—any way but the way she tried to do it. He seldom hugged her or showed her any affection; he seemed far more interested in her older brother and his activities. He'd often tell her, "You should try to be like Bill; he's really got his act together."

On the other end of the family, her younger sister seemed to get all of the attention and babying. Little Joyce was Baby Princess and could do no wrong, and big brother Bill was the fair-haired Knight of the Family Round Table. Clarissa felt caught in the typical "middle-child squeeze." She became very good at pacifying, negotiating, mediating, and learning to "get along."

Clarissa's mother hadn't been much help. She was a fairly critical person herself. In many ways, Clarissa grew up feeling as if she were under scrutiny and criticism a great deal of the time. She could handle it from her mother, but her dad devastated her with withering sarcasm.

"Even when I did something well, he'd say, 'Finally, Clarissa does something right. Will wonders never cease?'"

I was curious about how Clarissa had gotten on so well in the business world. One clue was that she was the first-born *girl* in her family and had the typical competitive drive that comes from trying to keep up with an older brother who is a real go-getter. Possibly Clarissa's competition with her older brother, Bill, had given her the ambition to do well in the workplace. When I asked her how she felt about the treatment she received on the job, it turned out she had been very lucky. She had started at the bank soon after getting married in her mid-twenties, and during the first few years had been fortunate enough to be under two women supervisors who were understanding and easy to work for. And now that she was manager of a local branch, she served under a vice-president who genuinely liked and respected her. Yet at home Clarissa lived in fear, guilt, and anxiety. By day she marched through her job with surefooted confidence; by night and on weekends she walked on eggs.

"What I can't understand," she wondered, "is why I'm always taking the blame for everything. Why do I always feel so guilty, when Jim is the one who is being irresponsible and inconsiderate?"

From Clarissa's description of Jim, he sounded almost like a misogynist of sorts—that is, a woman hater who is clever at shifting the blame and making his wife feel guilty for his bad behavior. In *Men Who Hate Women and the Women Who Love Them*, author Susan Forward advises the woman who may be living with a misogynist as follows:

Such men sincerely and convincingly argue that their outrageous behavior is an understandable reaction to some terrible deficiency or provocation on your part. By doing this, the misogynist avoids having to consider the possibility that he has some serious shortcomings. By shifting the blame to you, he protects himself in two important ways: he absolves himself of the discomfort of recognizing his role in the problem, and he convinces you that your character deficiencies are the real reason why you are having trouble together. Any criticism or questioning of him is immediately turned back on you as further proof of your inadequacies.[1]

Whether or not Jim was a full-blown misogynist was hard to say. We'll take a longer look at misogynists in chapters 9 and 10. What I tried to do for Clarissa was help her handle, and hopefully get rid of, her guilt.

"A likely reason you feel guilty and are convinced it's 'all your fault' a lot of the time is the criticism you got as a child. From what you tell me, your father drummed guilt into you with his constant complaints and put-downs. Chances are if you were around any man who wasn't approving and considerate, you'd feel you were the one to blame for whatever went wrong. You've been very lucky to work for supervisors who have let you blossom into who you really can be, but you've got to do something at home or it's only going to get worse."

"But what can I do?" Clarissa wanted to know. "Jim knows just how to press my buttons. He causes the rift, but I take the blame and apologize! Then he's real sweet. We usually kiss and make up and make love and everything's okay again. I know he's the one who should be apologizing, but at least it's a way to keep things on an even keel."

"Did you hear what you just said?" I asked her. "You are worried about keeping things on an even keel. You know that Jim is the one who is wrong but *you* take the blame and apologize because *at least* this is the one way to get some affection from the man you love. But what you need to understand is that we men tend to solve problems with our wives by having sex with them. The problem may go away for us, but not for our wives. Jim sounds like many of the men I see in my office—he solves his problems with you sexually."

"What do you mean he solves problems sexually?"

"Your self-talk script might run like this: 'My husband treats me without respect or consideration. It causes a problem. I get frustrated, possibly even angry, and then I feel guilty, as if it's my fault. In order to be loved, prized, held, and treated with affection by my husband, *I* apologize for *his* inappropriate behavior, and then we have sex and make up.' Clarissa, your husband is a controller and he can read you like the manual for one of the computers he works with. He knows just what buttons to push to keep you pleasing him while he does as he wants."

Clarissa's big brown eyes narrowed a bit and lost some of their warmth. I felt I was seeing her "bank face" in action as she geared up to handle a problem on the job. She was an extremely capable person and now that she saw the problem clearly, she wanted to do something about it.

"I have something I'd like you to try," I told her. "Why don't you start using some of the methodology and techniques at home that you often use at the bank during your business day while solving problems or handling situations?"

"I'm not quite sure how I'd do that," she responded. "Jim doesn't work for me. He's my husband, and when I go home I'm a totally different person."

"Try looking at it another way," I said. "For example, if somebody is irresponsible at work, or is late or careless, what do you do?"

120

"We have certain procedures we follow," she said matter-of-factly. I could almost see her mental gears shift back to the bank and how she operated there. "If somebody is late or a clerk loses a deposit, for example, he or she is given notice, and if it happens again, there are penalties."

"Well, why not try at home? When Jim is late for dinner and doesn't phone, tell him it's in the oven, or suggest that he send out for a pizza. But the big point is to *not apologize*. Quit blaming yourself when he causes a problem."

"Okay, I'll try it. It sounds simple but it isn't going to be easy."

"A lot of things are simple," I answered. "That never makes them easy."

Clarissa made slow progress with her new plan. The first few times she tried it, Jim managed to manipulate her with his controlling manner, and instead of being confident and assertive, she wound up blaming herself and apologizing. We had to work on Clarissa's guilt gathering, which didn't really surface until she had been in to see me two or three more times. It turned out she had pervading anxieties and fears that she didn't really deserve to get what she wanted, especially at home. She just couldn't make that jump from the workplace to what happened behind her front door. The minute she hit the porch, she slipped back into her "I've got to keep things going smoothly, everything depends on me" mode.

Jim was a classic controller and knew just how to work Clarissa's guilt buttons. When she tried to leave his dinner in the oven when he worked late, he said wearily, "It's been a long, hard day and now I cap it off with warmed-up leftovers. I didn't want to stay late—we were putting in a tough new program and the boss had to have it by morning. I guess I'll just skip dinner and go to bed."

Reverting to her old form, Clarissa was flooded with guilt when Jim acted as if she had done him a terrible injustice. She apologized all over the place and convinced Jim to stay up so she could cook him a mushroom omelette—one of his favorites. Somehow Jim managed to stay awake long enough to enjoy the omelette, and they went through their usual cycle of making up by making love.

"You get A for effort but C for execution," I told Clarissa when she related the incident at our next session. "Jim knows how to press your guilt buttons and get you to back off whenever you try to face him with his poor behavior."

"But he did have to work late on a special project," protested Clarissa. "I was being selfish by not holding dinner for him. . . ."

"No, you weren't," I told her. "Has Jim forgotten how to dial the telephone? The issue isn't that he had to work late. Anybody might have to work late now and then. The issue is that he never calls and lets you know. The issue is that he decides not to go on vacation with you and won't tell you until the night before you're to leave. The issue is he really isn't showing you respect and consideration, and that's what you're trying to get a little more of. You won't make any progress until you stop holding yourself responsible for Jim's well-being and happy feelings. What you've got to be more interested in is your own well-being and not having to experience these feelings of constant frustration and anger because Jim doesn't show you the same respect he'd show his fellow workers or his boss."

Clarissa left with renewed determination to make some real changes, but the next week she was back with another story of defeat. This time Jim had made it home for dinner but had copped out on doing his share of the cleanup, something they tried to divide evenly when they could because they both worked.

"He looked at me with that tired, accusing stare, and what could I do?" Clarissa, explained. "I know he's got a very tough job with a lot of pressure, and I had had a fairly easy day at the bank, so. . . ."

"So you let him win again," I said. "Clarissa, you're playing by Jim's rules. Whatever is convenient for Jim is right. The agreements, schedules, or plans the two of you make don't really mean anything. Jim lives by his own agenda. Why don't you look at it like a tennis game. When you serve, the ball has to go into the right service court. When Jim serves, the ball can go anywhere and still be 'in' as far as he's concerned."

At our next appointment, Clarissa reported a small victory. When Jim tried to cop out on his share of cleaning up after dinner, she calmly but firmly informed him that she had had a tough day, too, and that she had to get some books back to the library before it closed. She would see him later.

When she returned, the dishes were cleaned up and Jim was sitting watching television in a semi deep-freeze. But instead of apologizing or trying to get him to talk, she gave him a kiss and said, "The kitchen looks great!" Following that bit of encouragement (which I had urged her to give whenever Jim made even the slightest improvement), Clarissa got ready for bed. The next morning he was a bit cool but by the following evening he seemed to be his usual friendly self. Dinner was on schedule and cleanup was shared without incident.

"Congratulations!" I told Clarissa. "A journey of a thousand miles sometimes begins with those first steps toward the kitchen sink with the dirty dishes. But let me compliment you on your compliment to Jim when you told him the kitchen looked great after you got back from the library. You didn't give him a lot of saccharine, phony praise, but you did reinforce him by letting him know you noticed his effort and that you appreciated it."

Clarissa stayed in counseling for another month, making good progress while slipping backward on occasion. But I knew she had scored a real breakthrough when she told me about the Friday night she had invited another couple to dinner at 7:00 p.m. Jim called at 6:20 and said, "We've been working the bumps out of a tough program all day. We've almost got it, and if I can just stay another hour or so, we'll ship it for sure."

"Have you forgotten we're having the Marshalls over for dinner?" Clarissa asked.

"Well, I guess we did say something about having them over. But this is an awfully important program, Clarissa. You know how hard I've been working on it and if we can solve it tonight, it will help me relax over the weekend."

"I know it's an important program, Jim, but this dinner's important, too. I don't think I'm going to be able to relax if you aren't here to enjoy it with us. I'll expect you in half an hour."

With that, Clarissa hung up, and in half an hour Jim came through the door.

"And the best part," Clarissa said excitedly, "was that when he moped around and huffed and puffed because he didn't get his program done, I just said I understood how he felt, but we did have dinner guests coming and why shouldn't we try to have a good time? I didn't feel guilty, I didn't take the blame, and I didn't apologize!"

Clarissa was really catching on. She will probably always have the tendency to want to feel some guilt or take blame, but if she stops, steps back, and realizes what's really going on, it can change everything. I like to call it "calling an audible," the way a football quarterback sometimes changes his play at the line of scrimmage. If you hate football, you can call it anything you want, *as long as you get the respect and consideration you deserve.*

Whenever you're manipulated by controllers who want you to gather more guilt, your best defense is the cognitive self-discipline I talked about in chapter 4. Instead of buying into the manipulation and taking responsibility, feeling sorry, giving in, being a good sport, and so on, step back mentally and take stock. Ask yourself, *what is really going on here? What are the facts? What was the original agreement?* You don't have to be rude or mean or selfish. All you have to do is be rational.

Cognition means "thinking"—the mental process by which knowledge is acquired. Perception, reasoning, and intuition are also involved. Pleasers who grapple with guilt and an almost automatic reflex that has them taking the blame, making the apologies, and trying to take most of the responsibility for every situation, usually lack a clear perception of themselves and the people who are controlling them. Cognitive self-discipline will help you see a clearer picture of what is really happening.

One thing is certain: Whenever a pleaser becomes a guilt gatherer, you can be sure there will be people around her who are guilt dispensers. In our next illustration, we will meet Georgia, who gathered guilt for different reasons than Clarissa. In this case, it wasn't her husband but her five sons who controlled her, and who decided to make it rough when she got remarried to Rob.

This Stepfather Was Getting Stepped On

Georgia had darting eyes. As we talked, a diamond of at least two carats sparkled in the light while she nervously tapped the edge of the sofa and kept looking around the office. Five years before, at age forty-six, she had been divorced when her oldest son was sixteen and her youngest was nine. Her five boys were now ages fourteen to twenty-one.

Her first husband, Jon, was a physician and surgeon who had left her for another woman. The divorce had been a quiet one and Jon had given her ample child support and alimony to make life comfortable for her and the boys, all of whom stayed with their mother. But despite the financial support, Georgia had a tough time helping her sons understand why their dad had left.

When she met Rob, Georgia thought a lot of her troubles were over. On a sensitivity scale of 1 to 10, with 10 "highly sensitive," Rob probably would have scored 9.6. From Georgia's description, Rob was anything but a controller. He sounded like a tender, caring man, and he and Georgia should have been very happy, except for one thing: the five boys.

"My sons decided from the very start they didn't like Rob. He's a lot different from Jon—not as forceful or macho. He's actually sort of a mellow, easygoing type. I guess my boys think he's not manly enough, or something. . . ."

"It's not unusual for children to dislike a stepparent," I reassured Georgia. "Making any remarriage work with children involved is a tough job. People in stepfamilies can expect to be stepped on."

"Well, Rob is getting stepped on, all right," Georgia confided. "They have their friends over to the house at will without asking either of us. They give Rob all kinds of cheap shots, and they help themselves to his clothes and personal things. They also use him financially and keep asking for money. I guess the last straw was when they were rude to him in front of our friends the other night. Enough is enough."

"Where are you in all this? Rob is probably reluctant to say anything because they are really your sons. . . ."

"Well, I try to keep things as happy and smooth as I can," Georgia went on. "The boys were hurt badly when Jon left and we got the divorce. I just don't feel I have the right to say much to them now. . . ."

"What I hear you saying is that you feel guilty about what happened five years ago, and you're being permissive with your boys to make up for it."

"I suppose you're right," said Georgia, as she continued to drum nervously on the arm of the sofa. "But what can I do now? Rob is becoming alienated and definitely feeling used and put-upon. The money isn't the point. He's well-to-do, but he doesn't like being taken advantage of."

"For openers, I'd start tightening up on the boys just a little bit. You have many characteristics of a pleaser. You don't like to make trouble. You want to keep things smooth. Let's do a mini life-style quiz on you, and then next time you come in, I'd like Rob to come along, if he will do so."

Georgia's mini life-style showed that she was an only child, extremely perfectionistic and eager to please. Her father had been fairly loving and affectionate toward her, but he had died when she was six. Her mother had never remarried, and Georgia had always tried to be a "good girl"—very obedient, always toeing the mark and living by the rules.

"I'm afraid you fall into the category I call 'guilt gatherer,'" I told her. "You don't like to make mistakes. You like to play by the rules. When your first husband left you for another woman, you blamed yourself. You probably thought it was your fault—maybe you weren't sexy enough or attentive enough. Now you have remarried and you find yourself between a rock and a hard place. You feel guilty about the divorce and you're letting your boys get away with things that they should be brought up short on, and fast. Frankly, they need a little Reality Discipline. They should be made responsible for their actions. Now that Rob is getting turned off, you're probably worried about losing him. . . ."

"You're right," she admitted. "That's why I came to see you. I just don't know what to do. I keep feeling that this whole thing is my fault."

"You're involved, but it isn't necessarily your fault," I said. "See if you can get Rob to come in, and we'll all talk together at your next appointment."

Rob was happy to come in and turned out to be more than willing to work on the problem. What struck me was that he and Georgia were strongly committed to their marriage and making it work. He admitted he had been hurt by the way the boys acted and the fact that he didn't get any backing from Georgia, but he said he understood.

"If the two of you can come together on this and create a united front to the boys, you've got a good chance to turn things around," I observed. "Georgia, what you have to do is quit letting guilt be the propellant for some very poor decisions. Of course your sons suffered when Jon left and there was a divorce, but you suffered also. What you're doing now by feeling guilt over this is continuing to suffer, sort of paying penance for what you think was your fault."

"Okay, how do we get started with dealing with the kids?" Georgia wanted to know.

"Well, we could ship them to a nice boys' camp somewhere in Siberia for the next five years, but that probably wouldn't be too practical. Instead, I suggest that you take out that word *no*, dust it off, and start using it more. The boys have to learn that, no, they can't have the car whenever they want, no, they can't borrow Rob's golf clubs or tennis racket, no, they can't wear his clothes and, no, they can't 'borrow' money from him and not pay it back or be accountable for it. And above all, no, they can't be rude or disrespectful to him simply because he isn't their 'real dad.'"

"That's going to be a tall order," Rob injected. "Some of the boys are pretty strong willed."

"Well, that's where you two have to come together to form a strong union. I often say that in their way, children are the opposition. They work as a team, and unless you two come together as a team, they'll tear you apart. In fact, that's what they're trying to do anyway. Sad enough to say, they don't really want your marriage to work and they hope they can split you up."

"I wish there were something I could say to them that would help them understand," Georgia said.

"There is. Georgia, I think you have to find those opportune moments when you can sit down with one son at a time and say, in effect, 'Hey, your dad left me—he left all of us. I know that hurts, but I have found happiness with another man and I want you to accept that for my sake. I'm coping the best I can with the hurt from the divorce, and I expect all of you guys to try to make the best of it, too. I need your help to make this a brand-new family, so please try to accept the facts as they are. I know that no one can replace your dad for you, because he's your dad, but Rob is really trying to accept you kids and I expect you to make every effort to accept him.'"

We set up some ground rules that Rob and Georgia felt they could comfortably enforce, and they went back home to try them out. Item number one was that Georgia would make Rob her first priority, and he would even come ahead of her five sons. Another ground rule was that Georgia had to stop being "middle person" between her husband and his stepsons.

"Avoid triangles," I told Georgia. "Communication should never go from your sons to you and then to Rob. For example, if any of the boys want to borrow his car, golf clubs, or fishing gear, you are no longer to say, 'I'm sure he won't mind.' Instead, try saying, 'Why don't you talk directly to Rob about that. He'll be home in half an hour.'"

The first few times she tried the new rules, Georgia got some interesting looks from her boys, but they shrugged and went through the motions of asking Rob's permission when they wanted to use some of his things. Another rule was no "borrowing" money without a distinct agreement on how it was to be paid back. In this case, Rob had to show a little more backbone himself, which he was glad to do once he knew Georgia would back him up.

Crunch time came when Rob told Chip, the sixteen-year-old, "No, you can't use the car because the last time you borrowed it, you brought it home below empty, and that was not according to our agreement."

Chip's response was not exactly full of gratitude and warmth: "Boy, you're getting awfully tight with your money and your car and stuff like your golf clubs. . . ."

Georgia was present and she "pulled the rug out" on Chip by letting him know that she would not tolerate any more talk like that to Rob, and that if Chip wanted to borrow any more money or use the car again, he had better apologize and be more respectful in the future.

It was tough sledding for several months, but this story has a happy ending. Rob actually developed a warm relationship with several of the boys, and they all wound up paying him more respect. This was one stepfamily where stepping on the stepparent stopped because Mom and Dad came together, put their collective foot down, and said, "We'll have no more of this!"

At one of our final sessions, Georgia admitted to me that it was especially tough when the boys tried to push her guilt-gathering buttons, which they knew so very well. They tried everything from "A real dad wouldn't act this way," to "I don't know why Dad left, but maybe I'm getting a hint."

But Georgia took all the shots, cheap and otherwise, and kept smiling through everything. She continued to struggle with guilt, but its grip was lessening. She understood mentally that it was senseless and nonproductive to continue to do penance for the divorce. But at the visceral or feeling level, she still had memories of Jon and that first family circle that had been torn apart.

"Consider selling the house you are in now," I suggested. "It's where the boys have grown up, I know, but it's also where you go to the closet to hang up one of Rob's shirts and automatically you're reminded of Jon."

Georgia and Rob took the advice, and a few months later they relocated in the same school district in a house with enough space to give each boy his own bedroom. Georgia is a pleaser who has seen the terrible power of guilt and what it can do to an entire family. Now, instead of gathering guilt, she works on gathering positive feelings about herself and her life.

What Makes the Pleaser Gather Guilt?

Guilt is a terrible motivator in anyone's life, but it is especially destructive when it works on the pleaser. Pleasers are often guilt gatherers for several reasons:

1. *They feel bad about past mistakes* (which can go all the way back to childhood) and feel the need to suffer to atone for their sins. They think, *Bad things only happen to bad people, so I guess I'm getting what I deserve.*

   I like Dr. David Burns' insights in *Feeling Good.* He says that the idea of being a "bad person" is central to guilt. We need to differentiate between healthy feelings of regret or remorse and the falseness of the unhealthy guilt trip. To feel remorse is to admit you did something wrong or hurtful which violates your personal ethical standards, but you don't distort this into concluding, "I'm a bad, evil, immoral character." As Dr. Burns puts it, "remorse or regret are aimed at behavior, whereas guilt is targeted toward the 'self.'" [2]

2. *They live according to the expectations of others,* which become their standard of right and wrong. What pleasers think doesn't matter—they couldn't possibly be right anyway. Pleasers live by the other person's rules, game plan, or agenda. This kind of destructive pattern is especially evident in many marriages, where the pleaser may find herself with an abusive

or distant man who keeps her "playing by his rules."
(*See* chapters 7 through 10.)

3. *Living by somebody's else's rules naturally leads pleasers to take responsibility and blame for most of what goes wrong.* False guilt drives the pleaser to automatically think, *It's all my fault. I'm always to blame!* Check yourself for how often you say, "I'm always . . ." or "I never. . . ." The psychological term for this is *overgeneralization*, and it's a great way to wallow in guilt. Whenever you overgeneralize, you leave yourself wide open for the pain of rejection. When people disagree with you, criticize you, or turn you down, your automatic reaction is to think, *I'm always wrong*, or *I never seem to do things right*. Overgeneralizing almost always leads to guilt—and more "pleaser misery."[3]

4. *Guilt gatherers would rather suffer than change.* Many pleasers go through life driven by guilt but not doing anything about it. It is actually easier for them to worry and be anxious about breaking old rules than it is to make new ones of their own and start living differently. One of the major hurdles for every client who comes to see me is *making the decision to really change.*

   Most people perceive change as more painful than the present situation. Pleasers may be in a situation that is unpleasant, frustrating, even maddening or dangerous, but at least it is *familiar*. The familiar is somehow safer and more desirable than the unknown of change, so pleasers put up with their problems. That's what Clarissa and Georgia did until something triggered them to take action.

Moving from Sick Guilt to Healthy Innocence

To tell the guilt gatherer, "You've got to stop feeling guilty," is not only foolish but it can be harmful as well. The person burdened by false guilt which she has gathered possibly all her life doesn't drop that burden in an instant. But for starters, the guilt gatherer can at least practice a premise of justice that has guided our nation and many other countries for centuries: "Everyone is innocent until proven guilty."

There are ways to move from sick and neurotic guilt feelings to a healthy "innocence" in which you are willing to give yourself the benefit of the doubt. Because we are all imperfect, we do make mistakes. We are guilty of certain infractions, we overlook things we should do, and do things we should not. What the guilt gatherer must try to do is recognize the difference between real mistakes and imagined ones, between real guilt and false guilt. Following are some ways to start:

1. *Drop your high-jump bar of perfection from nine feet down to something you can clear more easily.* One psychologist has said, "Guilt is . . . a disgust at falling short of the ideal self-image."[4]

   An *ideal* self-image is much different from a *high* self-image. I have an exercise I do with many clients in which I ask them to describe their ideal self versus their real self (see chapter 3). Ideally, we usually see ourselves as efficient, on time, neat, always loving, patient, kind, and on and on. If anyone faces overwhelming odds against living up to her ideal self-image, it is the pleaser who is usually a wife, mother, and holds down a job outside the home to boot.

Mothers are particularly vulnerable to guilt feelings, and they often make the mistake of putting the kids first and leaving little time for themselves or their husbands. I often tell women clients, "It might be easier to be Mother Teresa than to be a 'perfect' mother. Try being the most loving wife you can be and everything else will fall into line."

We'll be looking more closely at perfectionism in chapter 6, but suffice it to say that perfectionism is a major cause of guilt, and the sooner you can lower your standards of perfectionism, the sooner you can stop gathering so much guilt!

2. *Stop living by the other person's agenda and expectations.* You have a right to your own agenda and to set your own expectations for yourself. Let the other person take some responsibility to help make things go right. If the other person cares about you at all, he or she will do just that. We'll be looking much more closely at this principle in chapters 9 and 10, which deal with the Supersuffering Pleaser's relationship to the Super Punishing Controller.

3. *Stop beating yourself along with all those dead horses.* Sure, you have probably made some mistakes; you will undoubtedly make quite a few more. But agonizing over the past is useless, and worrying about the future is a foolish waste of energy.

4. *When you start to take the blame, "Call an audible."* Check signals, take a time-out, step back, and think it through. Ask yourself, *What would the "old you" do?* Next, ask yourself, *What is the "new you" going to do?* Answer these two questions accurately and you will feel less guilt and be far more pleased with your own behavior.

All of the above points are useful, but the most important is number one. "Stop gathering guilt" doesn't mean you must be perfect, that you must get everything under control, and *then* you can relax. In fact, the harder you work at being perfect, the more guilty you are bound to feel!

It may sound contradictory, but to get control of your "pleasing-itis," just let go. Admit your imperfections—better yet, *accept* them. It is not a question of *giving up* but of *growing up*, as we will see in the next chapter.

6

Pleasers, Perfectionism, and the Avis Complex

"I'll just have to try harder."

Another archenemy of most pleasers is their perfectionism, an insidious inner drive that I often label "slow suicide."

Let me underline the "inner drive" idea. Perfectionism doesn't come from the pressures without. Life's challenges don't force you to be a perfectionist. You are forcing yourself by continually raising the bar a bit higher, setting goals that are too ambitious, setting yourself up for failure and frustration and another ride on the pleaser merry-go-round. In *Feeling Good*, David Burns says it this way:

Perfection is man's ultimate illusion. It simply doesn't exist in the universe. . . . It's really the world's greatest con game; it promises riches and delivers misery. The harder you strive for perfection, the worse your disappointment will become. . . . Everything can be improved if you look at it closely and critically enough. . . . So, if you are a perfectionist, you are guaranteed to be a loser in whatever you do.[1]

What Are the Signs of a Perfectionist?

Perhaps you suspect (or think you know) you are a perfectionist. What signs do you see? How does a perfectionist actually behave, besides wanting to be perfect and always trying harder? I'd like to introduce you to three very different women who have perfectionism in common. Meet:

Carrie. Sixteen, pretty and pert, blue eyes, blonde hair, a spare 114 pounds on a 5'7" frame that could easily carry 10 or 15 more pounds. Her problem? She strives to please a family of perfectionists who constantly chide her for being "too fat." She is also a victim of bulimia.

Annette. Thirty-six (looks more like forty-six), mother of three, putting forty thousand miles a year on her minivan, trying to be the perfect supermom who always pleases her kids, her family, her entire world. But Annette is running out of adaptive energy, and she has only so much.

Jill. Thirty-three, a perfectionist who could qualify for Miss Avis Complex of the Year. The epitome of the pleasing woman, Jill feels she must be nice to everyone and keep everybody happy. The word *no* is not in her vocabulary. A first-born daughter, she runs her father's business with the precision of a Swiss watch. But behind Jill's forced smile is a great deal of rage and anger at her father, who never compliments her on her work, her children, who are too demanding, and her husband, who checks out to watch the tube every night.

Each of these women illustrates some of the most damaging and dangerous effects of perfectionism. The reason I say many pleasers are perfectionists is that the pleaser usually tells herself she only counts when she gets the approval of others. And what better way to get approval than to do things "right" and "perfectly"?

The pleaser wears her mask of perfectionism, and when congratulated on the perfect dinner party, the perfect outfit, or any other kind of perfect job, she says, "Oh, really? It wasn't very much—just something I put together at the last minute. . . ."

In truth, the "last minute" may have lasted all day or possibly the entire week for whatever she did to earn the compliments.

You Have Met the Enemy, and Guess Who?

Along with realizing that perfectionism comes from within, mark it down that the perfectionist is her own worst enemy. If you are a perfectionist to any degree, *you* are probably your most severe critic.

Sixteen-year-old Carrie's perfectionism had much to do with her development of bulimia which, along with anorexia, has become a near epidemic disease in recent years. The typical victim of these ailments is female, and often young. The victim of anorexia nervosa refuses to eat or eats very little, and usually doesn't eat in front of others. Her weight often dwindles to eighty or ninety pounds. Bulimia victims, on the other hand, are binge eaters who self-induce vomiting. They are more difficult to spot because they manage to maintain their normal weight. However, there are some people who are both anorexic and bulimic.

The plight of the anorexic or bulimic woman has been dramatized in several books, including *Starving for Attention* by Cherry Boone O'Neill, first-born daughter of pop/gospel music superstar Pat Boone.

A typical first-born child, Cherry was Mama's little helper as early as the age of four. As her younger sisters arrived, she took on more and more responsibility and developed a "good little girl routine" to help herself feel valuable, loved, and worth something. She remembers a piano recital when she was only four, and feeling guilt when she lost her place and couldn't go on.

She gathered more guilt when she felt responsible for injuries suffered by her sisters, Debby and Lindy, although in both cases it wasn't her fault. She became a "daddy's girl" and always did her best to please him.

As a young teenager Cherry became preoccupied with her weight and began feeling depressed because she was too fat. When her weight reached 140 pounds on her 5'7" frame, she started dieting in earnest, and then somehow the diet became an obsession. By the time she was a senior in high school, her weight had dropped to ninety-two pounds and she was skin and bone.

Cherry's alarmed parents took her to doctors who diagnosed her condition as anorexia nervosa. Her battle back to normal weight and a healthy outlook on life makes gripping reading. Cherry lists a number of contributing factors that took her down the road to almost starving herself to death, including: "high expectations, high visibility, perfectionism, overprotection . . . sibling rivalry, my perceived role as mediator between family members and unresolved grief."[2]

As Cherry says, these are the ingredients in a formula for self-destruction.

Carrie Was Killing Herself

When a young teenager named Carrie came in to see me, she was also on the road to self-destruction with the same kind of problem. In her mid-teens, with ash blonde hair and sparkling blue eyes, Carrie looked as if she could have stepped off the cover of *Seventeen* magazine, but she felt—and actually believed—she belonged on a fat farm. At 5'7" and 114 pounds, Carrie's problem was not weight. It was a totally twisted self-image that compelled her to go on food binges, "pig out," as her generation likes to call it, and then regurgitate "to be sure she kept her weight down."

After their family doctor drew a blank, Carrie's mother made an appointment for her daughter with me. It didn't take too many sessions to learn that Carrie's life-style and favorite line of self-talk sounded like this: "I only count when I'm perfect, get straight A's, and always cooperate." Carrie simply couldn't say no, especially to the significant people in her life.

And she couldn't say no to food. She would go on a binge, but then guilt would flood in and she would throw it all up as her way of doing penance for "being too fat." But when she threw up, she would still be disgusted with herself, because she knew it was senseless and destructive. Talk about a vicious cycle—Carrie was caught in one!

When we got into Carrie's family and relationships, I learned that her father was practically nonexistent in her life. Ever since Carrie could remember, Dad had been "busy at work." He spent little or no time with her and showed her very little affection.

141

The people in Carrie's family who did spend time with her included Uncle Bill, Grandma, and Mom. Grandma was an only child and Mom was a first born. Carrie was also the first-born daughter. If you have read the first five chapters, you already have this one figured out. Carrie got nothing but criticism, especially about being careful that she didn't get "too fat."

I suppose Grandma and Mom, perfectionists in their own right, were only trying to help by constantly chiding Carrie about keeping a nice figure, but what they managed to achieve was to turn the girl into a superpleasing perfectionist who was her own worst enemy and then some. The "then some" was her bulimia, which probably turned out to be a blessing in disguise because it caused the family to seek some badly needed psychological help.

What Carrie needed was not constructive criticism but love and encouragement—"psychological cradling" in the arms of those who claimed to care about her.

"Why do you think you'll get too fat?" I asked her.

"I just know it. Mom and Grandma and Uncle Bill notice when I gain even a pound. Besides, I know I am much heavier looking than Allison."

"Who is Allison?"

"My best friend—she's so tiny and has a gorgeous figure. Next to her, I look like a truck."

It turned out that Carrie was one inch taller than Allison, but Allison was three or four pounds heavier than Carrie! Obviously, Carrie was much more slender than her friend, but she simply wouldn't believe it. Carrie was convinced that she was already fat, ugly, and unattractive, and if she weren't careful it could get worse.

As I made *slow* progress with Carrie, I also worked with Grandma, Mom, and Uncle Bill in different sessions to help them understand that their "constructive criticism" was anything but constructive.

I counseled Carrie for just over a year, which is unusually long for someone who believes in offering short-term therapy. I would have preferred to see Carrie leave much sooner, but the Carries of this world need lots of encouragement.

Carrie's bulimia symptoms eventually dissipated, but I am afraid she will always struggle with perfectionism. She is in a long-term battle to overcome the programming she has received all her life to be feminine, pretty, and slim. Unquestionably, we live in a perfectionistic society, which demands an extra bit of perfection from girls and women. Like any teenager, Carrie was under tremendous pressure at school to be popular, cool, "with it," and attractive to the boys. When you add the tremendous pressure she received at home and had been receiving all her life, you can understand why she wound up with bulimia.

I find it very rewarding to work with young people like Carrie and help them begin to see themselves in positive terms. No one is perfect; we all have flaws. Zits are normal. Life has bumps and lumps, and sometimes they appear in inconvenient places. Only when the perfectionist honestly comes to grips with these realities can she stop torturing herself with a fantasy that simply can't become reality.

Perfectionists Destroy Themselves Bit by Bit

More food for thought for the perfectionist is that she doesn't have to have bulimia to destroy herself. Perfectionists often mistakenly label their compulsive "I've got to do it right" behavior as a "quest for excellence." In truth, excellence and perfectionism are poles apart. The seeker of excellence tries to do her best and is satisfied with a solid, honest effort. The perfectionist seeks to be the best and is continually frustrated and defeated because she knows she "could have done it even better if. . . ." The seeker of excellence gains strength and energy from the satisfaction of a job well done. The perfectionist exhausts herself playing the greyhound running after a mechanical rabbit called "the perfect performance."

In their provocative book, *Real World 101*, James Calano and Jeff Salzman talk about two distinctive approaches to excellence: *practical perfectionism* and *neurotic perfectionism*. The neurotic perfectionist feels she must be the best at everything she does—achieving the state of the art on every project. For the neurotic perfectionist, finishing a task or reaching a goal is almost impossible. No matter what it is, it will always need more work.

On the other hand, the practical perfectionist is committed to excellence, watches the details, and has good work habits. She also knows when to quit. The point is, you can spend too much time and energy on a lot of things. As Calano and Salzman point out: "When debating the benefits of a higher degree of quality in an endeavor, be sure you consider the energy required to achieve it. Look at it this way: when you get one thing done, you've created a space to do another thing."[3]

When Annette came to see me, she was a Played-Out Pleaser heading for depression and worse. "Type A behavior" is often a condition associated with men, especially hard-driving executives, but Annette acted like a Type AA in her first interview. She sat on the edge of the couch, spoke in short, staccato bursts, and seemed in a hurry.

"Do you have to be somewhere?" I finally asked.

144

"As a matter of fact, I do—I have to pick up my oldest son after his karate lesson, and it's five miles from here. Can we wrap this up fairly quickly? I came to you because I'm feeling so frazzled—tired all the time. Some mornings I wake up and think, *I just can't do it again, but I have to.*"

"What is it you *have* to do?" I wondered.

"I'm president of the P.T.A., teach all year in our Sunday school, and also belong to the local chapter of Junior League. In addition, I have a very demanding husband and three lively sons, ages eleven, nine, and eight. I'm putting forty thousand miles a year on our minivan covering all the bases, getting all of us to meetings, classes, lessons, clubs, and teams. I've almost lost track of everything that everyone is in. I just try to follow my daily list and hope I don't forget somebody one of these days."

"Okay, I get the picture on the *what.* Now let's talk about the *why.* Is this pace really necessary?"

"I've been asking myself the same question lately, but I don't see how I can slow down. It's all there to be done and I do it. I've always been a doer—that's what my dad used to say when I was a kid."

"And now you're doing everything to please your family?"

"You could say that, I guess. I know they take advantage of me, but I don't mind—at least I haven't until lately, when I've gotten so tired."

"How do they take advantage of you?"

"Well, Howard—that's my husband—thinks nothing of bringing home friends or clients to dinner without telling me. He also likes to make love in the middle of the night—just after I've managed to wind down and get to sleep."

As we continued, I learned Annette was an only child whose parents had both died when she was eleven. She had gone to live with an aunt and had struck out on her own just after high school. She had always prided herself on working hard, being dependable—someone you could count on. As she put it, "I've always liked to make people happy."

The first thing we did for Annette was consult with her family doctor to get a prescription for mild depression. My drug prescribing seldom goes beyond Tylenol, but in this case I could see Annette was almost exhausted, mentally a well as physically.

In following sessions, I explained to Annette how and why she was putting so much stress on herself and seriously depleting her supply of adaptive energy. In one of my other books, which I irreverently titled *Bonkers: Why Women Get Stressed Out and What They Can Do About It*, I discussed Hans Selye's General Adaption Syndrome and how a person's adaptive energy supply can be used up too quickly by too much "dis-stress" in life.

Selye points out that each of us is born with only so much adaptive energy, and when it is finally gone, so are we. In Selye's terms, when all of our adaptability is used up, "irreversible general exhaustion and death follow."[4] In other words, even a DieHard battery will eventually run down.

I didn't mention dying to Annette, but I did warn her to slow down. I also had a session with Howard and the three boys in which I told them, in essence:

"You know, Mom is in bad shape. She could be headed for serious trouble, maybe even some kind of breakdown. I think all of you need to think about what she does for you every day. You should write it all down and talk about it together. She's partially to blame for being so tired because

146

she gets overinvolved in your lives, but what do you guys do to make her life nicer?"

I asked Howard when was the last time he came home from work and said to Annette, "Honey, I will take care of the kids. Why don't you go do what you want to do?" Howard just blinked.

When I talked to the boys, it was quickly apparent that they had no responsibilities at home whatsoever. Again, Annette was partially to blame for this, but Howard also needed to get in the picture and start doing more fathering.

The first time I talked to Howard and his sons, they all expressed shock and a little bit of anger. The boys were particularly selfish. They had never been trained with any Reality Discipline that would make them feel more responsible for their own actions and have concern for others. They weren't worried about Annette's physical or mental well-being. They were more concerned with, "Who's going to make our breakfast this morning? Who's going to do our laundry? Who's going to get us to baseball practice?"

Eventually, I got through to them. While Howard was a controller, he also had a strong sense of fairness, and once he realized Annette was carrying far more of the load than she should, he moved in with his controlling nature to change things, and fast. The boys were given chores and responsibilities. Howard stopped bringing people home for dinner unannounced. Everyone started pitching in, and in two months Annette was off her medication and back functioning with a new set of rules that said, fundamentally, "Mom is not the chief slave, cook, and bottle washer in this family. She is a person, and we must seek to please her as much as she tries to please us!"

In essence, Annette had been living with four takers, and she had been the only giver. They had surrounded her like vultures and were taking small pieces of her, a bit at a time. The pleaser-perfectionist can destroy herself, or let others destroy her by simply wearing her away. To live an ultraperfectionistic life-style is like taking a huge chisel to the corner of a building and giving it one good shot a day. Someone might walk by and say, "What are you doing?"

You could reply, "I'm knocking down this building. . . ."

The other person might laugh and say, "It'll never happen. That will take forever."

The truth is, however, that eventually it *will happen*. A shot a day does wear a building—or a perfectionist—away.

A Perfectionist Can Sometimes Be a Pain

One more good reason to abandon perfectionism, or at least try to get it under control, is that your family and friends will love you more for it. Many pleaser-perfectionists find themselves between a rock and hard place. They want to please; they work very hard at pleasing twenty-four hours a day, but at the same time they find themselves "getting on the case" of their spouses, children, or colleagues. In a sense, these perfectionists are "pleasers in reverse," controllers who can make life miserable for everyone within earshot.

The perfectionist is caught in a web of her own high expectations. Because she expects so much of herself, she likewise expects a great deal from others, and the result is that everyone—the perfectionist included—slowly goes bonkers.

Thirty-two-year-old super pleaser Jill, perfectionist to a "P" and a first-born daughter, had married at age twenty and had four children by the time she was twenty-eight. For the past seven years she had stepped into being secretary, office manager, and general girl Friday in her father's insurance business. In effect, she ran her dad's business for him so efficiently that he spent a great deal of time trying to bring his golf game into the low eighties.

At first impression, Jill came across as "very together." She had striking black hair and was very neatly and smartly dressed. Unlike Annette, she showed none of the impatience of a Type A personality. In fact, she came across as a very relaxed, sensitive woman who would make a good wife or friend.

After a few more sessions, I found another Jill behind the quiet smile and sensitive demeanor. Her sensitivity to others was really designed to hide her real feelings, which could be summed up in one word: *anger*. Jill felt she had to be nice to everybody, that it was her lot in life to please everyone.

She particularly went out of her way to please her father, hoping to hear an occasional "nice job" for her work with him at the insurance office. Nothing pleased Jill more than being told she had done a good job, but in seven years of running the family business, her dad had never said one word of encouragement or praise.

"I knock myself out to do a good job at the office, and sometimes I have to neglect my own family to do it," Jill said bitterly. "Some days it seems as if everyone wants a piece of me. I run the office as smooth as silk, but the stress gets me uptight. So by the time I come home, I'm ready to blow. I dump on Manny and the children which, of course, makes me feel guilty—as if I'm not a good mom."

One other pressure on Jill was a neighbor with children approximately the same ages as hers. Jill would be devastated by reading the bulletins the children brought home from school announcing that her neighbor friend was active in many of the P.T.A. affairs. She was also a den mother for Jill's younger son, which only made Jill feel worse because she was not spending time doing that kind of thing.

It was apparent that Jill had a gigantic Avis Complex. She was trying harder to please her father at work and not succeeding. She felt the need to try harder at home, but was finding little time to do it.

Jill's husband, Manny, wasn't much help. In stereotypical male fashion, he came home each day from his job at the plant, ate dinner, and checked out early, while Jill had to continue covering all the bases. First she worked all day, then picked up the two younger children at the day-care center, came home, and got dinner going.

"I imagine the five o'clock piranha hour is pretty rough," I commented. "The kids all seem to want to take a bite out of your flesh right about then, don't they?"

"You have my kids pegged pretty well. Actually, I guess I'm a pretty permissive mom. I tend to let them get away with things because I feel guilty about being away at work all day. And then I try to get them involved in a lot of activities to make up for my not being there."

It turned out that Jill was like a lot of perfectionist mothers who believe their kids need "their young horizons expanded." When Jill listed the activities of her kids, it sounded like the horizons had gone past the horizon:

Her eight-year-old son was in Little League and soccer, plus Cub Scouts, karate lessons, and a model-car club. He was planning to start saxophone lessons next month.

Her seven-year-old daughter was taking ballet and gymnastics, besides being in Brownies and taking piano lessons.

Her five-year-old daughter was a little "me too," and also took ballet and gymnastics and piano. On many days of the week, Jill was running around throughout the dinner hour getting her kids to various lessons, picking others up, and so on. The result was that she often got behind, rushed, and irritable. She snapped at everybody, including Manny, her husband. But everybody in the family knew that Jill was a paper tiger, and all they had to do was weather the storm and she would finally leave them alone and still do everything herself.

Manny was an only child who had been doted on by his parents and grandparents. Because the women in his life had always catered to him, he expected the same treatment from Jill. As a father, Manny was there but was not very involved. Sometimes he would play catch with his son, but he left most of the parenting to his wife.

Jill felt guilty about Manny's bailing out as a father, but at the same time she often refused to allow her husband to do certain things that she claimed she wanted him to do. For example, her seven-year-old daughter, Rebecca, started pestering her to go on a special shopping trip to look for dresses. Jill complained, "Manny doesn't lift a finger to help with the children. Why can't he take Rebecca to look for dresses?"

To everyone's surprise, Manny planned to leave work early to take Rebecca on a special shopping trip after school. Somehow Jill found out and rescheduled her entire day so she could take Rebecca shopping herself. Her reasoning? "Men don't know anything about little girls' dresses, and besides, Manny really needed to do some important errands and repair jobs around the house."

After hearing that story, I began wondering just who was the pleaser and who was the controller in this particular marriage. What was clear was that Jill was a perfectionist who couldn't delegate much of anything.

Perfectionism was driving Jill to try to do it all. She knew (or thought) she had higher skill levels than Manny in many areas. Because he would sometimes forget assignments, she seldom asked him to pick things up at the store; she simply did it herself. She would justify her failure to delegate simple jobs to her husband by saying, "I can do it better, and anyway, if you want something done right you might as well handle it yourself."

I finally got Manny into counseling, and when I informed him that parenthood wasn't just women's work and that his wife really needed him, he was a mixture of surprise and frustration.

"Well, even if I want to get involved, what will Jill let me do? I've always felt a little bit like the fifth wheel. Jill runs everything."

We worked out a new schedule, especially for the children. I gave Jill my standard piece of advice for parents with children and too many activities: "Cut each child's activities to only two a year. That will broaden their horizons quite nicely and you'll be money—and peace of mind—ahead."

Jill agreed to try it. She was using up her adaptive energy fast, and while her constitution had been able to cope to that point, eventually she would have reached the exhaustion stage.

As important as it was to get things straightened out in her immediate family, perhaps the biggest step forward was getting Jill to level with her father at work. Her dad was a self-made perfectionist—a man who had pulled himself up by the boot straps and built his business from scratch. He was the type who believed that people shouldn't get special praise for doing their jobs. After all, they are paid to do their jobs—that's enough.

Because his daughter had always tried to please him as a young girl living in his home, it was easy for Jill's father to continue the syndrome when Jill came to work for him after establishing a home of her own. She needed the job and the extra money, but she needed something else even more. I pointed out to her that she had never really made a break from her father. She had never really "left home" mentally or emotionally. By working for him, she was still playing the role of the little girl from the past who wanted to please her demanding, perfectionistic daddy. The only difference was that now, instead of getting his slippers, she was preparing the profit-and-loss statement and handling clients.

"You need to face your dad and tell him how you feel," I told Jill. "Here you are, practically running a million-dollar business by yourself, and being grossly underpaid to boot. You need to do three things: (a) be honest with your father, (b) clear the air once and for all, and (c) ask for a hefty raise."

It took some time, but Jill did work up the nerve to face her dad. Like many controllers, once confronted he backed down and made some adjustments. He raised Jill's salary from twenty-six thousand dollars a year to thirty-eight thousand dollars a year. With the extra money, Jill was able to hire a combination housekeeper/baby-sitter, which made care of the children a lot easier. She was able to find a woman in her early sixties who was just itching to care for children, and her grandmotherly personality was a perfect match for Jill's kids.

To say that Jill's life today is "a piece of cake" would be far from the truth. There are still many stresses and demands upon her, but at least she has learned to step back and take a more objective look at what she is doing. She's allowing Manny to get more involved in the family and their marriage. And, her new relationship with her dad is a much healthier one. He isn't taking her for granted as much and, while he will never become a great giver of compliments, he does occasionally tell his daughter he appreciates her work.

One of the keys to helping Jill change her life-style and cut back on her perfectionism was showing her that she was setting her goals far too high. In fact, her goals were out of sight. I believe a good rule of thumb is that *goals should be just out of reach, but never out of sight*. We all want to stretch ourselves with worthy goals, but taking on too much can turn your "to do" list into a tyrant. You wind up trying harder and harder and enjoying it less and less.

Semi-Easy Steps to Accepting Imperfection

We have looked at several ways perfectionism can make life miserable for us and our loved ones. Following are steps you can take to learn how to "become imperfect." There is much you can do to change your behavior and try to be just "a little more average," as you get your perfectionism under control.

1. *Realize you are the only one who can control your perfectionism.* Notice I say "control," not "eradicate." That little girl who grew up to learn to be a perfectionist is still in there. She keeps whispering that you should try harder, run faster, and do more. You must take your little-girl self firmly by the hand and inform her that she is off base. You don't *have* to do more and more in order to be "perfect." You will *choose* to do enough, and that will be it.

For example, try lowering your standards just a bit. Instead of aiming for 100 percent, deliberately try for 80 percent, 60 percent, or even 40 percent. Dr. David Burns gives his clients this advice and adds, "See how much you enjoy the activity and how productive you become. Dare to aim at being average! It takes courage, but you may amaze yourself!"[5]

2. Women like Jill say, "But if I drop my standards, I'll go to pot and so will everything else." *Don't be afraid that lowering your standards will turn you into an irresponsible slob.* The typical perfectionist can lower her standards a bit, but totally lose them? Never!

In fact, it will help others become more confident about approaching and relating to you because you won't seem so invincible. You may wind up with more friends who can relax when you're around.

3. *Deal with your perfectionism in tiny steps.* Perfectionism can destroy your life one blow at a time, but you can change your behavior slowly and steadily by not trying to do too much too fast. The old saying has it that "great cathedrals are built one brick at a time." You can build your new life-style the same way.

4. *Along with taking tiny steps, never look at the whole picture and try to change everything immediately.* In other words, don't say, "I've got to stop being a perfectionist and I'm going to stop *today*." If you try to quit your perfectionism "cold turkey," you undoubtedly will fail. Then you will get discouraged, give up, and go back to your old comfortable (but still painful and destructive) routine. In fact, give yourself the right to make a few mistakes. I have quoted Dr. David Burns' fine book *Feeling Good* at several points, but I'd like to share one more excellent piece of advice that he calls, "Why it's great to be able to make mistakes."

1. I fear making mistakes because I see everything in absolutist, perfectionistic terms—*one mistake and the whole is*

ruined. . . . A small mistake certainly doesn't ruin an otherwise fine whole.

2. It's good to make mistakes because then we learn—in fact, we won't learn *unless* we make mistakes. No one can avoid making mistakes—and since it's going to happen in any case, we may as well accept it and learn from it.

3. Recognizing our mistakes helps us to adjust our behavior so that we can get results we're more pleased with. . . .

4. *If we fear making mistakes, we become paralyzed*—we're afraid to do or try anything, since we might (in fact, probably will) make some mistakes, then we are really defeating ourselves. The more we try and the more mistakes we make, the faster we'll learn and the happier we'll be ultimately.

5. Most people aren't going to be mad at us or dislike us because we make mistakes—they all make mistakes, and most people feel uncomfortable around "perfect" people.

6. We don't die if we make mistakes.[6]

5. *Start with a small corner of your life, one aspect you know you can control.* Perhaps you want to quit riding your family so hard. Say to yourself, *This morning, when the kids do their chores, I will keep my mouth shut and I will not follow along behind them and do them over.* Then, stick to your vow no matter how hard it might be to leave the house with the beds slightly wrinkled, the blouse not quite straight on the hanger.

Also, refuse to be the timekeeper who takes the responsibility of making sure the kids are on that school bus. Quit running through the house shouting, "It's eight-ten! I'm telling you, you're going to miss your bus!" Then, a few minutes later: "Are you ready yet? The bus is coming . . . it's eight-fourteen!"

Instead, let your kids be responsible to make the bus themselves. I know this won't be easy. Moms tend to think their kids will *never* make that bus, but with only sixty seconds to go, children have a way of flying out the door—not necessarily in perfect, every-hair-in-place condition, but they *do* make the bus—somehow.

And what if they miss the bus? Don't come to the rescue with car keys in hand! Let them ride their bikes or walk to school a few times. They will either enjoy the exercise or they'll get themselves out to the bus stop on time. You only have to pull the rug out once or twice and they get the idea!

6. *Another strategy you might want to try is leaving your house "slightly imperfect," with something out of place.* You don't have to make your home look as if a cyclone hit it. I'm talking about a misplaced magazine, a chair not in its usual spot in the corner—anything to help you visibly, actively, and consciously practice *not* being perfect. Again, I emphasize that you should not worry about becoming irresponsible and profligate with this new behavior. All you're trying to do is provide a safety valve, a little space, that will help you feel less stressed.

Granted, the first few times you try to leave the house a bit imperfect or try not to come along behind everybody else and do their jobs over, you may feel more stress, not less. This is only natural because you're trying to break an ingrained habit that has taken all your life to develop. You will feel temporary discomfort, as you might when you start wearing a new pair of shoes. But stick with it, and eventually you will see some results. With practice, your new life-style will feel like your favorite pair of slippers.

I realize that the above suggestions could be called "gimmicks" and that not all of them may work for you. That's okay. Try them, as well as some of your own ideas, and *use what works.* What you are after is to become more aware of when you are taking on too much, getting your priorities out of kilter and riding yourself, your loved ones, and your friends too hard.

7. *Speaking of priorities, keep a careful eye on your list making.* Most perfectionists carry lists to keep track of their lives. The "to do" list controls the perfectionist's life. To keep a lot of unnecessary items off your "to do" list, try developing a new approach to setting priorities. When opportunities come your way—offers to serve here or "try this" or "take that on," try pulling out a mental slide rule and asking yourself, *Where does this request on my time and energy rank in my life right now? How important is this? Is it something that will contribute to our well-being, or will this be a drain on us?*

8. *Balance your self-criticism with self-encouragement.* In other words, go easier on yourself when you goof, and even be willing to laugh at yourself now and then.

And make a real effort to be a little kinder to yourself when you do something well. Most perfectionists are programmed to seldom give themselves strokes unless everything is absolutely perfect and correct. Even then, the perfectionist will seldom openly congratulate herself. She is more likely to say, "It's okay, I guess. I could have done it better if I'd had more time." Even when she succeeds, the perfectionist might have a tendency to cheapen or discount her achievements by telling herself, *I got lucky . . . I don't know why they think mine was any good. . . .*

Quit using this kind of deadly self-talk. Stop making excuses for your success. Instead, start enjoying it!

Seek Excellence, Not Perfection

As I mentioned earlier, the perfectionist is never satisfied, never finished, and the result is that she is constantly living at varying levels of frustration and unfulfillment. By contrast, the seeker of excellence finishes a job, is satisfied with it, and goes on to the next challenge without a lot of self-judgment and self-criticism. In chart form, the comparison between the perfectionist and the pursuer of excellence looks like this:

Perfectionists	Pursuers of Excellence
reach for impossible goals	enjoy meeting high standards that are within reach
value themselves by what they do	value themselves by who they are
get depressed and give up	may experience disappointment, but keep going
are devastated by failure	learn from failure
remember mistakes and dwell on them	correct mistakes, then learn from them
can only live with being number one	are happy with being number two, if they know they have tried their hardest
hate criticism	welcome criticism
have to win to keep high self-esteem	finish second and still have a good self-image[7]

If perfectionism is a problem for you right now, your life is out of balance. What you are trying to do is "right the ship" a little bit at a time. Keep in mind that the balance must come from the inside, not from without. You must be your own gyrocompass. You correct your own course and get your life on a stable axis.

That's why I am so strong on balancing the spiritual aspect of life against the mental, emotional, physical, and social. Without a speaking relationship with God, your loving heavenly Father who accepts you unconditionally, your perfectionism becomes a "god" and cruel taskmaster. In biblical terms, your perfectionism is like the Pharisees, always seeking to pick up the first stone and hurl it straight at your self-esteem and self-image. Perfectionism thrives on legalism, and vice versa. The pleaser who wants to free herself from the shackles of perfectionism seeks to live more under God's grace and less under laws and rules.

In the last three chapters we have looked at the many lies that are swallowed every day by the pleasing woman who can't say no:

> I don't see a way out . . . nothing is going to change . . . I can never win . . . everything I do seems to be wrong . . . they'll find fault whatever I do . . . they do it better than I do . . . it's never going to change . . . nothing I can do will make any difference . . . it's all my fault . . . it must be me . . . I've got to try harder . . . I've got to keep my family happy.

Bombarding yourself with the above kind of self-talk is guaranteed to give you low self-esteem, all kinds of "guilties," and an Avis Complex that can keep you running on the treadmill of perfectionism. Start taking steps toward imperfection today. Always be ready to reassess where you are. When you fail and slip back into your pleasing, perfectionistic ways, don't let it defeat you. Even realizing that you have slipped back is progress. Eventually, you will start to build that beautiful cathedral of a new and freeing life-style that will be positively pleasing to everyone—including you!

PART 3

How Pleasers Marry for Better and Often Live with Much Worse

Possibly the most common marriage partnership is that of the pleasing wife and the controlling husband. Unless the pleaser understands how to deal with him, she may be in for frustration—even misery. The next four chapters describe the controller—how to spot one before marriage and how to cope with one after the "I do's" have died away. Whether your goal is survival or just balancing up the power scales a bit, this section is rich with tips on

- understanding why pleasers find controllers so intriguing
- how sex can spoil a budding relationship
- why a Super Controller is a poor marriage risk
- the danger in "just following your feelings"
- how women are still trained to think, *I'm nothing without a man*
- testing your man to see where he falls on the controller scale
- why you should beware if he "always has to win"
- the "mythical marvelous man"—is he out there?
- finding your way out of the Controller Swamp of Discouragement
- how pleasers control controllers in self-defense
- understanding the "please read my mind" syndrome
- why it may get worse before it gets better
- why you shouldn't ever try to go it alone

7

Pleasers Are the Moths, Controllers Are the Flame

*"It was so electric . . . our eyes met
and I just knew he was the one."*

Beautiful was the accurate word for Rosalee, who at twenty-eight looked all of nineteen. Her dark brown eyes complemented her almost-black wavy hair, which fell softly around her shoulders. Her perfectly understated outfit flattered her lissome figure just enough to be intriguing.

Like so many pleasers, Rosalee gave a first impression of being confident and together. A first born, she had followed a feminine Yellow Brick Road to a high-income profession and had become an acoustical engineer three years before.

She had planned to have it all—a great career, marriage, and children "when there was more time," but at the moment there had been Jack, a blond, six-foot-one-inch Adonis of athletic grace whom Rosalee found irresistible.

"Jack has the 'pecs' to be a Chippendales dancer," Rosalee said with a quick laugh. "He turned me on so much that I was the aggressor the first time we ever went to bed. I knew I wanted to live with him after dating him for only seven weeks."

And so Jack had moved into Rosalee's condo and they had spent another six months in idyllic sexual bliss. Jack, also an engineer in the aerospace industry, kept telling Rosalee that sex with her was like "lift-off at Cape Canaveral." Over those months the two of them launched their own rocket every night, sometimes more than once.

"It was a dream, a storybook, a fantasy," recalled Rosalee. "I felt loved, prized, and cherished. Jack was so caring and sensitive. It was wonderful."

If living together was this good, Rosalee and Jack decided, why not try marriage. They tied the knot in a civil ceremony, attended by only a few close friends, and rushed home to—disaster.

"Jack seemed to change as we walked out of the courthouse," Rosalee admitted. "He became critical, demeaning, and cruel. I knew I was in trouble when he got out of the car and walked into the condo ahead of me without even a word. I thought husbands carried wives over the threshold on their wedding day. All I remember is Jack telling me to order some home-delivered pizza because he wanted to watch a play-off game. I was crushed."

Rosalee remained crushed, and the marriage lasted less than a year. Jack, the sensitive, caring prince of the living-together arrangement, had become a slimy frog in wedlock almost overnight.

"How could he change that fast?" Rosalee wondered. "I was sure I had found the perfect man—the exact opposite of my father. It turned out he and Jack could be twins. I swore I would never be treated the way Mom had been treated—so how could I pick such a loser?"

"You would be amazed at how often it happens. I know it isn't much consolation, but I counsel many women like you. Let's talk about your background—your family. Describe your mother or your father for me."

Jack Turned Out to Be a Hypocrite, Too

Immediately Rosalee launched into what sounded, at some points, almost like a tirade about her father, a critical, sharp-tongued man who had always "lived by the book." Rosalee had grown up in a very strict and legalistic church that emphasized God's wrath against sin and seldom spoke of His love. Her father had ruled his family with an iron hand and had always been sure that his wife "submitted" to him, meaning that she never questioned anything he said.

Somehow Rosalee's mother had stayed in the marriage until Rosalee and her two younger brothers were all out of high school and on their own. Then she quietly left and filed for divorce.

"My father never beat my mother, but he could go into a verbal rage that you would not believe. I used to ask Mom how she could stand it and she'd say, 'He doesn't mean most of what he says. He's trying to live the way he thinks God wants us to. It could be worse. At least he doesn't drink.'"

165

"Did your father pay much attention to you?"

"Only when I started dating in high school. Then he seemed sure I was going to bed with every boy I went out with. If I got in five minutes late he would holler at me about the evils of fornication and being headed straight for hell if I didn't change my ways. My father always made sex sound dirty and wrong, but all it ever did was turn me off on him, the church, the Bible, everything. When I got out of the house and on my own, I never went back to church."

"How did you meet Jack?"

"I didn't go to bed with many men—Jack was only the second one. But with Jack it was so tender and special—at first—and then it was like he had been wearing a disguise and he just ripped it off. As soon as we got married he became as critical and overbearing as my father. The only thing missing was the religion. Jack grew up in a home where no one went to church. I thought that would be good because that way he wouldn't turn out to be a hypocrite. But he turned out to be a bigger hypocrite than my father. Why? How could he fool me so badly?"

"Because, Rosalee, a father's influence on his daughter lasts for life. As much as you hated his behavior and unloving ways, they made an indelible imprint on you. It's as if you were programmed to find a man to marry who would be like your father. You thought you were getting someone much different, but hard as it is to understand, you picked someone just like your dad. As unpleasant as some things are, we gravitate toward what is familiar. There were certain things about Jack that attracted you—the same things that were your father's good points."

"How do you explain why Jack could be so wonderful for more than six months and then change in literally less than twenty-four hours?" Rosalee wanted to know.

166

"Because until you got married, your relationship was highly sexual. You mistook passion for real love and intimacy. I've a little saying I call Leman's Law of Male/Female Relationships: 'Sex precludes intimacy in fledgling relationships.'"

Rosalee's beautiful dark eyes flashed with anger. "What does *that* mean? How much more intimate can you get than having sex?"

"A great deal. Physical intimacy doesn't always include emotional intimacy. In fact, it can prevent it. Real intimacy includes communication, caring, and sharing yourself in many other ways besides just physically. Jack came off as tender and considerate, but from the way you describe him, he's a classic controller, and controllers always know how to play a role to get what they want."

"You still haven't explained how he could change so fast. . . ."

"Because until the moment you said 'I do,' your relationship had been sort of a game. You had been playing house, but the wedding meant the real thing. As long as you were just living together, all of the eggs weren't in one basket. There was always the possibility of simply walking away. As soon as you became Jack's wife, the whole game was different. That's why he became so critical."

"Why would my becoming his wife suddenly make him critical?"

"The real Jack was not the guy who had been so 'tender and caring' before marriage. Before you got married you were his playmate, but he had an entirely different agenda for a wife. In a way you were his prize, and once he won you, he thought he owned you. His criticism was his way of polishing and adjusting you to suit himself."

Sex and Affection Are *Not* the Same

In the several months she spent with me in counseling, Rosalee learned how pleasers are often attracted to controllers in much the same way that a moth is attracted to a flame. As a first-born daughter in a family where the father had been extremely strict and demanding, Rosalee was almost automatically trained to be a pleaser. And she did not escape absorbing the classic problem of many pleasers. Despite her beauty, she had low self-esteem.

Rosalee knew she was pretty, but she didn't think she was very capable. She explained her raises and advancements in her engineering career by attributing them to her good looks and pleaser personality. "I'm a nice piece of furniture," she said. "I'm not there because they think I'm really good at what I do; they just keep me around for a decoration."

Due to rebelling against her strong church background, Rosalee had a great deal of guilt and was sure that if there was a God, He was definitely not happy with her. When she met Jack, his blond good looks and beautifully built body turned her on sexually the way no man had ever done before. She saw few comparisons to her father, who had always been a bit on the overweight and flabby side. All she knew was that here was the man of her dreams, and how could she be so lucky?

She never thought about carefully comparing Jack to her father, or looking for signs of the controller. And even if Rosalee had known the classic signs of a controller, it is quite likely she would have been blind to them in Jack's case because sex with him turned out to be so exciting. During the first months of her relationship with Jack, Rosalee put far too much importance on the "great sex." She did not understand that her needs as a woman included *much more than sex.*

In a relationship that depends primarily on sex to make things go, the man's needs are almost always put ahead of the woman's. In *His Needs, Her Needs,* a fascinating study of marital affairs and how to avoid them, Willard Harley describes the five major needs of women and the five major needs of men. Not surprisingly, they are all different.

Dr. Harley bases his findings on more than twenty years of counseling married couples, many of whom were caught up in affairs. During that time he has gathered over fifteen thousand questionnaires that deal with the sexual history and behavior of his clients. He admits that his five major needs for men and five major needs for women don't hold true for the entire population, but the needs he discusses are the ones that have come up most frequently.

While Dr. Harley hesitates to rate one need higher than another, it is significant that the first female need he discusses is affection and the first male need, sex. He observes that men often mistake "having sex" with "being affectionate." Most of the men he has counseled (and I will toss in most of the males *I* counsel) do not really understand a vital idea: "Women find affection important in its own right. They love the feeling that accompanies both the bestowal and the reception of affection, but it has nothing to do with sex."[1]

In other words, women need and want nonsexual affection *first*—and then sex will follow quite naturally and enjoyably. Men, of course, want sex first, and usually falling asleep follows. As Dr. Harley points out:

> To most women affection symbolizes security, protection, comfort, and approval, vitally important commodities in

169

their eyes. When a husband shows his wife affection, he sends the following messages:

1. I'll take care of you and protect you. You are important to me, and I don't want anything to happen to you.
2. I'm concerned about the problems you face, and I am with you.
3. I think you've done a good job, and I'm so proud of you.

A hug can say any and all of the above. Men need to understand how strongly women need these affirmations. *For the typical wife, there can hardly be enough of them.*[2]

Controller Jack had no concept or understanding of Rosalee's real needs. And at first, neither did Rosalee. Jack's muscular good looks "turned her on," and she was more than willing to go to bed with him after only a few dates. During those first months of living together, sex was exciting and Jack was seemingly sensitive and caring enough to make Rosalee believe he was truly affectionate and cared about her. But when they tied the wedding knot, Jack's real nature came out. His feigned caring and affection dissolved into criticism and attacks on Rosalee about anything and everything. He still wanted sex, of course, but now it was on demand, and with no regard for her feelings or desires.

One of the very unusual aspects of this marriage was that Rosalee stuck with it as long as she did. Despite being turned off by her religious training, she was still programmed to try to make the marriage work. But when life became intolerable, she divorced Jack. Operating true to controller form, he quickly moved in with a new girlfriend and enjoyed another tryst.

How to Spot a True Controller

The sad truth is that a real controller who cares nothing about the needs of others is a very poor risk *in any marriage.* And yet, pleasing women are drawn to controllers "like moths to the flame." I use the old cliché about moths and flames only to underline one basic warning: When you get near fire, you get burned. There are ways to detect a controller, and the best time to do it is before marriage. No matter how charming and attentive he seems to be, there will be telltale signs that are warning lights any sensible women should heed.

The pleasing woman should pay particular attention to the actions of her date, boyfriend, fiancé, or spouse. What he *says* is not anywhere near as important as what he *does.* The typical controlling male is very good with words, but a woman must see through the forest of words to find the real tree, so to speak.

So, rule number one is this: *Watch the behavior, and don't put tremendous importance on the words.* That is not to say you shouldn't listen carefully to words, and one of your main goals is to see if your male companion is a man of his word. A major characteristic of controllers is that they play fast and loose with the truth. In fact, many of them are skilled liars. At best, they always see the situation through *their* eyes, never yours. And, of course, only what they see is "the truth."

When you match the characteristics of the controller with the characteristics of the pleaser, it's not hard to see why pleasers wind up doing all the pleasing and getting little in return.

The Pleaser	The Controller
Low self-esteem—always working hard to please and earn acceptance.	Capitalizes by keeping the pleaser off balance—in her place. He knows her soft spots, her Achilles' heel.

The Pleaser	The Controller
Often from a family that did not meet her emotional needs—particularly her father.	Incredibly, the pleaser seems inevitably drawn toward a man like her father—the "familiar" is somehow more attractive than what could be fulfilling and comfortable.
A fixer and reformer—she knows she can change him.	His "weaknesses" are what make the relationship go. If she could really "fix him," he'd probably be dull and uninteresting.
Tendency to fantasize—failure to grasp reality.	He seems to have a firm grasp on reality and everything else—especially the pleaser.
Quick to take the blame—she "knows it's all her fault."	He is quite willing to let her play the blame game—as long as she is always the loser.
Thankful for small favors—life could be worse.	He knows she'll put up with him—in fact, he's counting on it. He knows he's "got her in his pocket."
Has the Avis Complex—always trying harder.	And as she "dances on eggs," he plays the tune.
Doesn't feel worthy of real love or respect.	He knows he can lie and be overbearing and demanding because she'll take it—she "expects it."
God is nonexistent or a distant, dangerous judge or policeman who disapproves of her most of the time.	Since controllers like to play God, she is playing right into his hands.

How to Really Get to Know a Man

According to Willard Harley's list, communication is one of the five major needs in a woman. And one of the major complaints I hear from my women clients is, "He won't talk

172

to me . . . I want to hear about his day, and I want to tell him about mine, but all he says is, 'It was okay. Let's watch the news.'" Many marriages consist of two people who watch the same TV set but never get to know each other.

When I talk to some women clients about "really getting to know a man," they smile indulgently. They think I sound as if I need some remedial work in "Birds and Bees 101." Many of them say, "Well, you know as well as I do there is only *one* way to get to know a man."

Wrong. In fact, going to bed with Prince Charming on the first or second date is almost a guarantee that you won't get to know him very well at all. Oh, he'll get to know your body, all right, and vice versa, but he'll probably skip right past your mind and, more important, your soul. As for *his* mind and soul, the door will stay closed and the blinds drawn.

As Rosalee concluded her counseling, naturally the subject turned to where she would go from here. Because I am paid to give people counsel, I am not shy about bucking the trend that began some years ago as the "New Morality" and turned into a tidal wave of the same old immorality that has been around for thousands of years.

"My advice comes in two parts," I said. "One, wait at least four years until you remarry. Two, stay out of bed."

"Yes, I remember what you said about sex preventing real intimacy, but every man wants to go to bed," she protested. "I'll lose anybody worth having unless I'm willing to sleep with him."

"On the contrary—a man worth having will respect your wishes and desires and will not want to take you to bed after one, two, or even many dates. I'm old-fashioned enough to believe sex is for the intimacy of marriage."

"Oh, come on, doctor—these are the nineteen eighties. If I start using that line, everyone I know will laugh at me."

173

"Rosalee, I know that most of society rejects what I am saying. But take a look at the divorce statistics. The average marriage lasts seven years. Why do you suppose that's true? I believe one reason is that many marriages lack emotional intimacy because there was too much sexual action too soon. A healthy marriage has complete emotional intimacy that includes sharing, caring, mutual respect, communicating, trusting, being trusted. Intimacy is knowing each other at a much deeper level than the skin."

Rosalee bought my advice—at least most of it. She didn't quite make it to three years before remarrying, but I didn't mind. Actually, I tell women to wait four years in the hope that they will last two. But Rosalee did stay out of bed, and she found a caring man who respected her feelings.

In fact, Rosalee discovered that the more she said no, the more he pursued her. I got an invitation to the wedding, and at the reception she told me, "You were right. It was hard, but if I hadn't taken your advice, I never would have found Barry."

Love Is Not "the Tinglies"

Rosalee learned, through her bitter experience with Jack, the difference between real love and what I call "the tinglies." Far too many marriages are entered into with little more going for them than that electric euphoria generated when eyes meet across the room, table, or bed.

In America, especially, we pride ourselves on being free, independent, and able to decide things for ourselves. Marriages aren't arranged by parents anymore; children grow up, start dating, and are allowed to be adult enough to make their own choices about a mate. According to the statistics, they are batting around .500, which is great for building a career in baseball but lousy for building a strong nation with stable families.

Through television, films, pop songs, videos, slick "liberated" magazines, and romantic novels with any degree of steaminess you care to endure, young people (and not a few older ones) are being taught to "just follow their feelings." One enchanted evening they will meet that stranger across the crowded room (or singles bar), and be spirited away to lifelong bliss.

I am for freedom and independence as much as anyone, but my caseload says something has gone very wrong with the "just follow your feelings" plan. When the New Morality came into vogue, there was a lot of talk by so-called experts about the "refreshing new state of open-mindedness" we had reached. Wasn't it wonderful to rise above the puritanical, Victorian hang-ups of yesteryear and be open and honest about sexual relationships for a change?

A very unoriginal but laser-accurate saying is, "History repeats itself." Over the centuries, we humans have been awfully good at "correcting" something we believe is wrong and tossing the baby right out with the bathwater. In this case, the baby was common sense and the kind of morals and ethics that result in fair treatment for everyone, especially women.

It doesn't take a Phi Beta Kappa to figure out that the so-called New Morality is really the same old male approach to keeping women in the role of the submissive, pleasing sex object they can use at their convenience. My advice to women—and men—is this: In these open-minded days of the New Morality, "Don't be so open-minded your brains fall out."

175

What Could I Tell These Collegians about Sex?

Recently I was invited to speak to a group of 750 fraternity and sorority leaders at a major university in the Northwest. What could I tell them that would be interesting as well as helpful for building a fulfilling life? During eleven years as an Assistant Dean of Students at the University of Arizona, I learned firsthand that calling typical college students "sexually active" could be the understatement of the year. And if they aren't sexually active, sex is certainly on their minds.

Because I have never been known for being cautious, the thought came to me, *Why not give these collegians some good reasons they should say no to sex before marriage.*

I also am not known for having a very dignified speaking style. To open my talk on sex for this college crowd, I ambled to the podium after my introduction, and without bothering with "how happy I am to be with you," I said, "What do we call penises in our society?"

A decided hush fell upon the room. The young men who had been slouching in their chairs, expecting to be bored by a psychologist in a three-piece suit, were suddenly on the edge of their seats. Some were nudging one another, and I heard somebody near the podium whisper loudly, "Did he say what I *think* he said?"

From that point, I had their *complete* attention. Amazingly enough, when I finished, they gave me a raucous standing ovation, and many of the guys clapped harder than the girls!

When I got home Sande asked me what I had talked about. I told her I had spoken to fraternity and sorority people and had given them seven points to ponder:

1. *Sex precludes intimacy, especially when a relationship is new or just beginning.* I know the "new man" pictured in women's magazines is supposed to be a fascinating conversationalist who is interested in a woman's mind as well as her body, but a word of warning: If you give him your body too easily, the "fascinating conversation" may dwindle to grunts such as, "C'mere, baby. . . ."

   I recall a cartoon of two women sitting in a singles bar, gazing at a gorgeous "hunk" across the room. One woman says to the other, "Yeah, a good body is great to watch, but it usually loses something when you turn on the audio." Be sure to give your man plenty of opportunities to "turn on the audio" and tell you who he really is and what his values really are.

2. *Sex outside marriage ruins a good relationship.* I often use the analogy of ripping a piece of silk or other fine material. The male approach is very predictable. If he rips his silk dress shirt he tosses it to his wife and says, "No big deal, just sew it up."

   Whether she sews it herself or has it repaired, the point is that the world's finest seamstress can't mend the rip completely. It is always there—always marring the shirt.

   The relationship between a man and woman is much like weaving a fine garment. To bring sex into the relationship long before its proper timing is to rip and mar the garment. Oh, you can "sew it up," perhaps, and many couples do, some more successfully than others. But I see many women in my office who tell a tale of marital discord that can be traced right back to the tremendous pressure from the man to have sex too soon.

The pressure that sex too soon can bring to a relationship may be something as simple as concern about pregnancy. For a society that has supposedly solved pregnancy problems with sophisticated methods of birth control, there are an awful lot of unwanted pregnancies popping up (no pun intended). One problem is that passionate, physical lovemaking doesn't always lend itself to stopping to insert a diaphragm or putting on a condom. It is ironic that society seems to have suddenly discovered condoms because of the AIDS scare.

"At least wear a condom and don't risk dying" is the message in the new ads appearing in print or on TV screens. All this sudden concern about condoms is not caused by fear of pregnancy—it is fear of dying a slow, horrible death. Lost in the panicky din about AIDS is a real point: *Sex is not something to be done recreationally or as a way to get to know each other.*

Counselors across this nation are listening to the sad tales of woe from countless women who bought into the classic male line that essentially said, "Let's hop in the sack, baby, and get to know each other." This kind of controlling doesn't even deserve the label of garbage. Sex is the most intimate pact into which any man and woman can enter, and it should be reserved for the committed arena of marriage.

3. *Casual sex (sex outside of marriage with someone who is sure he "loves you") can end up in a case of herpes or something much more deadly, such as AIDS.* A recent study has revealed that the number of women contracting AIDS from male sexual partners more than doubled from 1982 to 1987. In 1982, the first full year medical authorities kept figures, 12 percent of women diag-

178

nosed with Acquired Immune Deficiency Syndrome got it from male sex partners. Five years later, 26 percent of women getting AIDS were contracting it from men.[3]

4. *Sex can trap you into an unwanted marriage.* It is amazing how many people I counsel who were pregnant at the altar. While they went ahead with the wedding, there was a resentment and a reluctance that finally surfaced years later in marital discord. Sex outside marriage plants seeds of distrust that can sprout in strange ways ten or fifteen years after the wedding day.

5. *Casual sex can lead to an unwanted pregnancy and being tempted, urged, or forced to have an abortion.* When I counsel a woman considering an abortion, I put aside my own strong convictions about taking an unborn but still human life. The debate over when life really starts and a woman's right to her body versus the child's right to life will go on indefinitely. The point I stress with all my clients is that experience has shown me that women who have abortions are undeniably risking all kinds of emotional havoc in their lives.

Proabortion advocates argue long, hard, and loud about the woman's right to make her choice, but they really don't have a whole lot of help to offer the woman who is haunted by guilt, the woman who unaccountably finds herself weeping at certain times of the year, when "the baby" would have just had another birthday. What would he or she have been like? Gone is the rhetoric about being free to choose; in its place is the awful reality and the ever-present, gnawing guilt.

6. *Sex before marriage can result in "flashbacks" years later when you are making love to your spouse.* I see flash-

backs regarding sex as analogous to the flashbacks one can undergo long after using a hallucinogenic drug. Picture it for yourself: There you are, married, deeply in love with your mate, and engaged in sexual intercourse, one of the most beautiful of experiences. Suddenly, out of your memory bank comes . . . Ralph (or Sherry or whoever). Remembering these earlier sexual partners not only can cause guilt but more important, it can interrupt or even seriously hamper your love relationship with your spouse.

7. *Love is not a feeling, it is a decision.* The concept of "just following your feelings" sounds attractive and even romantic, but is it really? The thought has occurred to me that if you and I decided to follow our feelings for just thirty days, we would undoubtedly wind up in jail. Try following your feelings for the next week. When on your way to work, if you feel like cutting somebody off, do it! If you are in a store and you see something you want, take it! Never mind the security guard standing three feet away from you.

These suggestions are absurd, of course, but no more absurd than "just following your feelings" when it comes to finding someone with whom you wish to spend the rest of your life.

I blush to admit that many people in my field—professional counselors, psychologists, psychiatrists—are in part responsible for the "follow your feelings" idiocy that has overtaken society. One of the major premises of the philosophy is that each of us must be fulfilled. To put it in the terms made famous by Abraham Maslow, we must be "self-actualized." There is nothing wrong with self-actualization. I'm for it, as long as some other items such as honesty, trust, faithfulness, and responsibility aren't tossed aside to reach the self-actualization pinnacle.

Love Is a Decision, Not a Feeling

Love is not a feeling. Love is not "the tinglies." Love is a decision that we must make every day to put someone else first in life. In a marriage, that someone else is your spouse. Love is a cognitive, willful act. Feelings have very little to do with it, particularly around three o'clock in the morning when the baby needs changing or somebody has "lost it" before getting to the bathroom to throw up. The scholars aren't sure if the apostle Paul was ever married, but he certainly had the definition of mature love down pat when he said this:

> Love is very patient and kind, never jealous or envious, never boastful or proud, never haughty or selfish or rude. Love does not demand its own way. It is not irritable or touchy. It does not hold grudges and will hardly even notice when others do it wrong. It is never glad about injustice, but rejoices whenever truth wins out. If you love someone you will be loyal to him [her] no matter what the cost. You will always believe in him [her], always expect the best of him [her], and always stand your ground in defending him [her].[4] (Bracketed pronouns added by the author.)

Not long ago I turned my car radio dial to "Focus on the Family" and heard Dr. James Dobson interviewing a young mother of two who was dying of cancer. She was explaining her feelings of despair and fear of what the future held for her children and her husband. To add cancer's cruel joke to her suffering, chemotherapy had robbed her of practically all her hair, but she went on to share that her husband didn't mind.

My eyes got a bit blurry as I heard her relate how he literally cradled her in his arms, gave her a kiss, looked right into her eyes, and said, "Do you know you are the most beautiful woman in the whole world?"

Here was a husband who knew love was *not* a feeling. Love is reassuring your wife as her life hangs in the balance.

Love is telling her she's beautiful, even after she has lost her crowning glory: her hair.

Love is unconditionally accepting your wife, holding her failing, frail body in your arms, and comforting her in the darkest of hours.

Love under this kind of pressure is the real measure of a man.

Love is warm, gentle, and tender . . . and it never fails.

Ignore the Warning Signs at Your Peril

According to Dr. Willard Harley, these are the five major needs of woman:

- affection
- conversation
- honesty and openness
- financial support
- family commitment

The five major needs of men, according to Dr. Harley's studies, are these:

- sexual fulfillment
- recreational companionship

- an attractive spouse
- domestic support
- admiration

In my opinion, the woman's key need is affection, the feeling that she is truly prized, loved, and cherished. Also extremely important is communication, the feeling that her husband is willing to listen to her and share at a deep level.

The man's key need is sex, followed closely by the admiration and respect of his wife. The "battleground" of sex versus affection (real emotional intimacy versus superficial sexual athletics) is where the pleaser must come to terms with the controller.

At the risk of sounding repetitive, the basic grain of the wood of your personality does not change. If you have grown up to be a pleaser, your inclination will be to please. If you have grown up to be a controller, that will be what you instinctively want to do in most situations. There is nothing wrong with being a pleaser, if you can be a Positive Pleaser (*see* the Pyramid of Pleasers on page 31). And there is nothing wrong with being in control of things and able to lead or take charge, as long as you are a "caring controller" who respects the rights and feelings of others.

To put it another way, if you are going to marry a controller, at least be able to recognize who and what you are getting and what kind of terms you need to come to in order to make a decent life together. Too many women who come to me for counseling were not able to recognize the signs, and now they are frustrated, desperate, and ready to bail out of the marriage.

Gwen was a case in point. She swore she'd never be like her mother because she had never gotten along with her while growing up. And yet as the years went along, she recognized that she and her mother had many similar traits.

As for her father, the pattern of the distant, unloving daddy didn't really fit. He had, in fact, been a very loving, caring parent, and Gwen had adored him as a child and throughout most of her teenage years. But right after graduation from high school, she met Larry and fell in love. Her dad, as well as her mother, was upset, because they didn't like Larry's manipulative, furtive manner. In a word, they knew instinctively he wasn't to be trusted.

"My dad and my mom saw through Larry a lot better than I did," Gwen recalled. "But I wasn't buying it. When my dad put a lot of pressure on me to break off with Larry, all that did was make me more determined than ever to marry him. We got married just after I turned nineteen, and my father refused to come to the wedding. I was heartbroken."

Gwen went on to admit that it took only a few months to prove her parents were right. Larry was not only a chronic liar and manipulator but he also liked to gamble, and would lose most of his paycheck in crap games after work. Gwen also learned that while in high school he had been arrested for shoplifting in convenience stores on several occasions.

"I'm living proof that the old cliché is right: Love *is* blind. Larry couldn't tell me the truth if his life depended on it. I can't believe I married him."

"I can," I told her. "It's hard to realize the tremendous impact parents have on our lives. For example, you admit you didn't get along with your mom, but now you recognize that you have many of her habits and characteristics. You did get along with your dad—in fact, what you're telling me says you adored him, but his disapproval of your love affair with Larry drove a wedge between you. What you

184

thought you saw in Larry was what you had always admired in your dad: strength, boldness, and confidence. Larry had confidence and boldness, all right, but he used it in negative ways to become a liar, a gambler, and a petty thief."

Unfortunately, attempts to get Larry into counseling were unsuccessful. When his dishonesty turned into adultery, Gwen blew the whistle. Larry's lying was simply too much to overcome. Her marriage met the same fate as Rosalee's, and for the same reason. Gwen and Larry had two and one-half strikes on them at the start, because she could not recognize the signs of the selfish and punishing controller. We will take a close and careful look at those signs in chapter 8.

Seeing Controllers "Up Close and Personal"

*"He's so wonderful . . . he has a few rough spots
but I can smooth those over."*

Why do pleasers often take the leap into marriage despite
vague feelings of uneasiness or clear warning signs that
tell them the relationship may have some real problems?
Why do they go ahead and marry for "better or for worse,"
only to find out that, sure enough, it was for worse? One
fundamental reason is that many women have grown up in
environments that have trained them to believe they are
"nothing without a man."

As recommended reading for my women clients, I often suggest Sonya Friedman's excellent book *Men Are Just Desserts*, in which she confronts the "I'm nothing without a man" problem head-on. As she analyzes what is still a prevalent part of our culture (despite all the strides made toward women's liberation and equality in recent years), Sonya makes the following points:

> As little girls grow up, they are trained by parents and society to believe they are incomplete and lack the capacity to take care of themselves . . .
>
> The woman is taught she must find a man who will "take care of her." She is the lesser half seeking the greater half, who can make her complete . . .
>
> A woman isn't worth much unless she marries. Then she is supposed to feel valued, but often doesn't feel that way at all . . .
>
> A woman typically rushes into marriage and gives up or postpones her own goals in order to support her husband's plans and ambitions. For doing this, she expects to be treated with devotion and respect, but often gets far less than she thought would be hers . . .
>
> Because the woman makes herself vulnerable to her husband, she becomes dependent on him. The less she is an autonomous, independent person, the more she needs from him.[1]

Instead of following this stereotypical path to disaster, Sonya urges women to see men not as the "main course" in their lives, but as "just desserts"—enhancements to an already complete and satisfying life in which a woman can make her own choices and take action on her own. As Sonya says, "When men are just desserts, you may choose to be in the arms of a man, but need never fear falling into his hands."[2]

How to Spot a Controller

Unfortunately, many pleasers do fall into the hands of controllers because they ignore, or aren't able to recognize, telltale warning signs or characteristics. Because controllers are often confident, "take charge" types, they can fool women into believing they are getting men who will be loving, caring, and affectionate. Instead, controllers turn out to be dominating, uncaring, and lacking the confidence to become emotionally intimate.

One of the most important steps any woman can take away from being dependent and "nothing without a man" is to learn how to spot a controller at less than ten yards—that is, when the controller gets close enough to intrigue or fascinate you. If you are just starting to develop a relationship, learning how to spot a controller may help you avoid making a painful mistake. If you are already married, it will at least help you understand the controller you married and how to deal with him.

Following is a little quiz I've developed to help identify the kind of controller who can cause the typical pleaser more than a little grief. Instead of answering each question with a flat yes or no, I suggest this scoring system: always, 4; often, 3; sometimes, 2; seldom, 1.

Telltale Signs of the Controller

_____ 1. Does he speak with disrespect or anger about other women who have been part of his life? For example, his mother, his sister, daughter (if previously married), employer, supervisor, and so on.

_____ 2. Does he have a temper—that is, does he get visibly angry or hostile?

_____ 3. Has he ever hit you, treated you roughly, or threatened to hurt you?

189

_____ 4. Is he a "flaw picker"—a perfectionist who is proud of his high standards, especially for others, and his "desire for excellence"?

_____ 5. Does he control or disapprove of your spending money but seem to have no problem spending it on himself?

_____ 6. Does he try to take advantage of you sexually, or make sexual demands upon you?

_____ 7. Does drinking alcohol—even a modest amount—start to bring out a "different kind of person"?

_____ 8. Does he make excuses for his drinking behavior, which often becomes excessive?

_____ 9. Does he use or enjoy humor that puts down or degrades others in subtle—or not so subtle—ways?

_____ 10. Does he lack the ability to laugh at himself?

_____ 11. Does he find it hard to apologize, or does he often make excuses for his behavior?

_____ 12. Is he "in control" where he works—that is, does he run the show, operate independently?

_____ 13. Does he often complain about employers or supervisors who "don't know what they're doing"?

_____ 14. Does he always have to win in sports, table games, and other competitive activities?

_____ 15. Does he usually "get his way" in deciding when and where you will eat, where you will go, what you will do?

SCORING:

50-60 A Super Controller who will be hard to deal with on any basis, long or short term.

40-49 A "typical" controller who quite possibly can be confronted and asked to change.

30-39 Shows a balance between control and flexibility, probably a good bet for a husband.

29 and under Probably not a controller, but look harder if he scored higher than a 2 on questions such as 1, 2, 3, 5, 6, 7, 8, 11, 14, or 15.

Keep in mind that quiz like the one above is too brief and general to be conclusive, but it can give you some important clues to help you start asking questions that will throw some more light on your relationship. Let's take a brief look at each to understand its significance and value.

1. *Does he speak with disrespect or anger about other women who have been part of his life?* A telltale sign of a controller is a man who feels his mother or older sister dominated him. Because he felt controlled growing up, he thinks it's his turn now. Harder to spot is the controller who was brought up by permissive parents. He could always "walk all over" his mother and now has little true respect for women. His lack of respect may not be evident in the early dating stages, but it will come out later when he lets down his guard.

Also, if your man has been married before and has children, *particularly daughters*, note very carefully how he treats them. Does he show them affection and real interest? If their mother has custody, does he make a sincere effort to see them? If not, beware.

2. *Does he have a temper—that is, does he get visibly angry or hostile?* This can be a somewhat misleading question because some people are capable of being very angry but not showing it. In most close relationships, however, such as dating, the engagement stage, living-together arrangements, or marriage, it is difficult if not impossible to conceal your anger from your partner. Watch your man in action: What makes him angry? Can he handle irritations in traffic? What happens when things don't go right, you are late, and so forth?

3. *Has he ever hit you, treated you roughly, or threatened to hurt you?* At many points I have mentioned pleasers who have to "walk on eggs" because of a husband's explosive temper. The controller often uses his anger to manipulate and control those around him. He knows that rather than

191

buck him they will tread softly to keep things smooth and peaceful.

If you are dating a man and he hits you, grabs you, and jerks you around roughly, or even threatens to hurt you, *immediately run, do not walk, to an exit to this relationship.* You probably have a Super Controller (possibly a misogynist) on your hands, and to continue the relationship will only lead to pain and suffering.

If you are already married and are experiencing this kind of violence, get help from professional counselors, your pastor, etc. Many cities have telephone hot lines the abused wife can call for help. My advice to a woman is to take her children and try to find a safe place to stay. That may mean bunking with Mom and Dad (if they live in town). It may mean going to a women's shelter.

The best bet for the abused wife is to go where her husband cannot find her. While she waits for him to cool down, she can plan her next move. If she believes that she wants to contact her husband, she should always meet with him in the presence of a third party. Unless a wife is a martial-arts expert, she must be careful to do everything she can to protect herself. She should not count on being able to talk sense or reason with anyone who outweighs her by seventy-five to one hundred pounds and is in all probability much stronger.

4. *Is he a "flaw picker"—a perfectionist who is proud of his high standards and his "desire for excellence"?* I talk to many pleaser wives married to controllers who complain that even when they jump a little higher and give it their best, their best isn't quite good enough. A rule of thumb I have seen through the years is that the pleaser perfectionist usually turns her perfectionism upon herself; the controller

perfectionist will find an outlet for his perfectionism at work, but come home and flaw-pick his family to death.

A controller might tell a woman she is "just perfect" before marriage. But once the knot is tied, the woman cannot possibly meet the controller's standards and expectations for continued and even greater perfection. Keep in mind that while many perfectionist controllers talk about their high personal standards, often what they are really saying is that they have high standards *for everybody else.* And if everybody else doesn't meet those standards, they will be quite unhappy.

5. *Does he control or disapprove of your spending money but seem to have no problem spending it on himself?* The perfectionistic controller is usually (in fact, I'm almost ready to say *always*) tightfisted with his money. In earlier chapters we looked at several case studies in which the husband controlled the wife through keeping her on a very tight budget, making her put up with the unrepaired washer, and so on.

If you are dating or engaged, observe how your man handles money and how he approaches the subject. Does he spend money as generously on you as on himself? Does he ever make remarks about how you "seem to think money grows on trees"? It may be done in a kidding or humorous way, but if your relationship is serious and definitely moving toward marriage, it won't hurt to have some frank discussions of how money will be handled in the family.

For example, I am a firm believer in joint checking accounts. A marriage is not a business partnership in which each partner has his or her own account and refers to "my money." In marriage, it should be "our money."

If you are married to a tightfisted controller who is making life anything from uncomfortable to downright miserable with his financial manipulating of you and the entire family, the same rule of frank discussion applies. Perhaps you will have to do as Sally did concerning her broken washer. Just call your controlling husband's bluff by phoning the repairman, and take it from there.

6. *Does he try to take advantage of you sexually, or make sexual demands upon you?* If you're still dating or in the engagement stage, go back and reread my old-fashioned comments about saying no to men who want to take you to bed before marriage. Have some honest discussions with your man about physical intimacy versus emotional intimacy. Does talking about emotional intimacy make him nervous or impatient? Does he even understand the difference between affection and "having sex"?

Reread the earlier comments from Dr. Willard Harley's book *His Needs, Her Needs*, where the difference between affection and sex is clearly defined (see page 169). A sure sign of the controlling male is the man who wants to have sex on demand, and he usually demands it very early in any relationship he has with a woman.

It is significant and encouraging that the New Morality tide shifted a bit during the later 1980s. In the spring of 1987, Abigail Van Buren devoted an entire "Dear Abby" column to the subject "It's Smart to Keep Saying No to Sex." Several young men wrote in after Abby ran a letter from a seventeen-year-old girl who had lamented the criticism and pressure she was getting for saying no to sex before marriage. She was beginning to wonder if she was weird and if she had to have sex in order to make a relationship last.

One twenty-year-old man wrote in to say he had been dating the same girl for two years and she was still a virgin. He had tried to talk her into going to bed with him, and had even dropped her a couple of times, but he always went back because of his strong attraction to her. He realized what a prize she was and that he was now quite ready to wait until marriage. His letter closed by saying, "Sex can cheapen a relationship, not make it more valuable."

Another twenty-year-old young man wrote to tell the young woman that she was "not weird for wanting a relationship with a guy without having sex. There are plenty of attractive, available guys who don't really care about scoring." And he added, "Today, the risks of sex far outweigh the pleasures."

A twenty-two-year-old college senior wrote in to say he was also a virgin, that the young woman was "not weird but unusual." And he observed, "It does not take experience to know that having sex is no substitute for making love."[3]

If you are already married and your husband's sexual approach has all the finesse of King Kong, you can go on putting up with it, or you can speak up. Let him know that "foreplay" is not something done on golf courses; it is usually done in bed by lovers who care about their wives' feelings, not just how good their bodies feel.

Let your husband know that while he may be able to sit around watching TV all evening and suddenly "turn on" at eleven o'clock, you do not. In fact, by then you are probably exhausted from having to do all the cleanup from dinner, put kids to bed, and so on. As I've said in the title of another book, *Sex Begins in the Kitchen*—when a husband shows his concern and love for his wife by helping with the chores and showing interest in all she has to do to keep the home functioning.

Let your husband know that he can't expect you to feel loved, prized, cherished, and sexy if you are the constant recipient of his put-downs and cheap shots.

Let your husband know that when the two of you have an argument, or worse, a fight, "making up sexually" doesn't really resolve anything. Men try to solve problems sexually but women want to solve them honestly by dealing with the issues.

7. *Does drinking alcohol—even a modest amount—start to bring out a "different kind of person"?* The controller can be one kind of person sober, but just a few beers or one or two cocktails and his nasty, vulgar, critical side comes out to play. I am not talking about the quantity of *what* he drinks as much as what happens *when* he drinks. I've had many wives tell me in counseling that after a few drinks their husbands "say things I just couldn't believe he'd ever say!"

8. *Does he make excuses for his drinking behavior, which often becomes excessive?* My rule of thumb for every woman is, "If a man has to drink every day—stay away!" If you are beginning to establish a relationship with a man and you notice that he seems to need a drink often—in other words, at some time during the day, or perhaps several times a day—don't excuse it by saying, "Well, he's under a lot of pressure and this helps him relax." The whole point of his drinking is to control the pressures of life. The excessive drinker (or drug user) drinks to escape from his problems.

If you are married to an excessive drinker who is controlling you and everyone else in the family with his drinking (and quite probably his alcoholism), you must get help for him as well as yourself immediately.

Phil Donahue dedicated an entire hour of his talk show to discussing the phenomenon of the "enabler" who continues to live with the alcoholic, making excuses for him, covering for him, and so forth. On the program were alcoholics, drug addicts, and their spouses, who had played the role

196

of enabler. Also present was a medical doctor who was the director of a drug-abuse treatment center.

The consensus of all present was that the enabler is not only playing a losing game but she is also becoming a bigger part of the total problem. As long as you are willing to play "Florence Nightingale" for your alcoholic or drug-addicted husband, he will let you. You must get help, and fast.

For starters, call your local Alcoholics Anonymous chapter and get a list of resources in your community. Choose the help that best fits your situation. You may need to go straight to an intervention program; perhaps your first step should be a support group. Maybe you need both. I highly recommend Al-Anon as a support group for wives and other members of the alcoholic's family.

9. *Does he use or enjoy humor that puts down or degrades others in subtle—or not so subtle—ways?* The controller is often good at creating "fun" at the expense of others, particularly his date, girlfriend, or wife. He can be sarcastic and satirical, but it is always at someone else's expense. The controller can be adept at the fine art of the "funny put-down" as he subtly sets up others to look stupid.

If you are just establishing a relationship, the put-downs may be subtle, but they are still there. It's "all in fun," of course, and he is "just teasing," but look for the pattern. For every "just teasing" put-down, is there a sincere uplift or compliment? Speaking of compliments, does your male partner give you many? What kind of compliments are they?

10. *Does he lack the ability to laugh at himself?* This question ties closely to question 9. The controller who likes to make fun of others seldom is capable of laughing at himself. He will usually pout or become irritated or angry if the joke is on him. Obviously, when you are being laughed at, you

197

are not completely in control. Of course, someone who is mature can laugh at himself with ease because he does not take himself that seriously. Controllers, however, take themselves *very* seriously.

11. *Does he find it hard to apologize, or does he often make excuses for his behavior?* Early in a relationship, the controller may take a stab at apologizing, but even then it is evident that he does it with reluctance or in a way that leaves him "not really wrong or that much at fault." Once married, the controller may never say he's sorry and, of course, his wife is "always wrong." Controllers are skilled in giving excuses for their behavior, explaining why things went the way they did, or claiming that "people really don't understand me." When they do apologize, it is probably for manipulative purposes.

12. *Is he "in control" where he works—that is, does he run the show, operate independently?* Controllers often find their way into occupations where they are "in charge" one way or another. Perfectionism pays off in jobs such as accounting, engineering, architecture, computer analysis, surgical medicine, anesthesiology, dentistry, and so on. Through his occupation, the controller learns to be more and more exacting and more and more in control. He literally gets better at it as he grows older. But the problem is, when he walks in the door at night, his perfectionism works against him and his family.

13. *Does he often complain about employers or supervisors who "don't know what they're doing"?* The controller who does not wind up on top of the heap, or cannot operate autonomously, will often find fault with any authority or supervision. He has the habit of moving from job to job because he "never gets the right treatment" or his "talents

aren't used correctly." He is often quite bright and verbal, a Mr. Know-It-All with an opinion on everything.

As a little boy, he learned to shirk his responsibilities and blame others for his own inadequacies and shortcomings. It is quite likely he was brought up in a permissive home where he could justify his behavior. Just as pleasers learn to please in childhood, controllers learn to control at an early age. The "little boy of the past" he once was he still is.

14. *Does he always have to win in sports, table games, and other competitive activities?* Does a simple game of tennis turn into a John McEnroe tirade at center court? Does a "friendly" game of golf, croquet, Scrabble, or Trivial Pursuit become anything but trivial? It is one thing to be a "keen competitor"; it is quite another to have to win at any price. If your man's motto seems to be "Winning isn't everything, it's the *only* thing," think about that—hard. How does that relate to you?

15. *Does he usually "get his way" in deciding when and where you will eat, where you will go, what you will do?* If you aren't married yet, check this one carefully. Some controllers can act very agreeable and seem to want to give you your way—"anything your little heart desires." But notice how he acts when the decision is fairly significant and it's a matter of his being inconvenienced, having to take second best, or doing something he would really prefer not to do.

What happens when your male partner doesn't get his way? Does he tend to pout or withdraw? Does he let you know that you have disappointed him? Do you find yourself apologizing and taking the blame (something you may do quite naturally—review chapter 5)?

A major characteristic of the controller is that he is "in control." I belabor the obvious only to point out that you should carefully watch your male companion to see how he operates. Is he unpredictable? Does he keep you "slightly off balance"? Does he usually get his way about where to go, what to do, what channel to watch? He may be quite subtle about it, but look back over any number of decisions the two of you supposedly made together recently. Who really won?

Another mark of the controller is that everything is geared toward him. He is the center of his universe, and you are one of his satellites. If he can't get his way by being slightly disappointed or possibly even "slightly depressed," he may try the other end of the spectrum and yell and scream. Controllers are experts at making their wives, fiancées, or girlfriends "walk on eggs." By now you may be so skilled in walking on eggs you feel ready for an appearance on Ed McMahon's *Star Search* show. Controllers must be kept happy at all costs and, believe me, the woman pays a high price indeed.

What Happens When You Ignore the Warnings?

Suzanne, thirty-one, was a divorcée with a five-year-old son when she met David in a singles bar. David seemed to be the epitome of everything Suzanne wanted in a man. The minute she mentioned her son, Tommy, David wanted to meet him and "take him bowling or something."

"We just hit it off immediately," she told me. "I was particularly impressed that he didn't want to take me to bed on our first date."

Suzanne went on to say that David waited a full month before he took her to bed. Then he moved in and stayed with her and little Tommy for three years. During that time she literally bankrolled his new business. Once the business was established, he dumped her and left.

Suzanne had come to see me in a state of shock and outrage. She thought David was "Mr. Right" and now she was devastated. Also devastated was Tommy, who had become closely attached to David, the only "daddy" he had ever known. Tommy's real dad had left when he was still an infant.

To cap the entire sorry tale, not long after David left, Suzanne received a call from a private investigator representing a client in another part of the United States. This woman had been married to David and she had hired the private eye to track him down so she could try to collect back-due court-ordered alimony and child support for the last three and one-half years.

Suzanne had not only picked a controller but he turned out to be something of a sociopath as well. Suzanne wound up out thousands of dollars, three years of her life, and a significant amount of adaptive energy due to all of the stress she endured.

"What happened?" she wondered. "How could I be so stupid? How could he seem to act so nice, so right, and be so wrong? During the three years he lived with us he was always gentle, attentive, and a very good lover."

"David sounds much more clever and manipulative than most controllers," I told her. "You set yourself up for him by making several tactical errors: You say he impressed you by waiting an entire month to have sex with you, but I say that was still far too soon. In addition, you let him move into your house in a living-together arrangement but with 'no downpayment'! You thought you knew David, but the relationship was still more physical than anything else. While David seemed to be a nice guy, you never really got to know him, did you?"

"I guess not," Suzanne admitted bitterly. "When the real David stood up, it was to march out the door and leave us high and dry."

"When I say he made no down payment, I simply mean you never got married. You had no legal rights and David took full advantage of that by draining you financially to get his own business going. And because you trusted him, you took no legal precautions to protect your interests in regard to financing his business. You just gave him what he wanted out of love, and he took you for all he could."

"But how could I have known?" she wondered. "What could I have done to check him out?"

"Did David admit he was married before?" I asked.

"He mentioned something about his first wife but that he had been divorced years before because she was 'a real witch,' as he put it. He told me nothing about owing alimony and child support. In fact, he inferred he had never had any children."

"How was David at handling money?"

"Well, he had his money and I had mine. I knew he was struggling to get his business going, so I kept loaning him substantial amounts. He would always say thank you, but come to think of it, he never did say much about paying me back."

"Did David drink at all? And if he did, how did it affect him?"

"David really didn't drink much—he had a beer now and then. He'd get a little silly, but that was about it."

"What kind of sense of humor did David have? Was he good at being sarcastic and satirical?"

"Now that you mention it, he did have a way of putting people down, but he was usually so funny nobody seemed to mind."

"What would happen when the joke was on David?"

"He never liked that. One of the few times he got really angry with me was when I made fun of an awful tie he was wearing while we were out with some of our friends."

"Tell me a little bit about this business you financed for David. Had he been in business for himself before?"

"Not that I know of. The reason he wanted to set up his own jewelry shop specializing in cubic zircons was that he had never been happy working for other people. He'd often say, 'Working for other people is stupid. All they want to do is take advantage of you.'"

"Who usually made the decisions when David lived with you? For example, if you went out to have some fun, that sort of thing."

"David always talked as if he wanted me to give my opinion, but he usually got his way in the end. I remember one night when I insisted on having Chinese food and he sulked the whole time."

"Even though you describe David as being a very gentle, caring person during the time he lived with you and your son, what you tell me proves he displayed a lot of controller characteristics. In addition, he obviously could lie and manipulate with the worst of them. I would have to see David in person to make a final judgment, but it is my guess, Suzanne, that he comes very close to being a sociopath—the kind of person who seems warm and wonderful but who really has no conscience. David was a great guy on the outside, but a Super Rat on the inside."

"Well, it's not hard to see that now, but I still keep wondering how he could fool me so badly and what I can do in the future."

"One thing to think about is that you went to great lengths to keep things smooth and be sure you pleased him. Is that a fair assessment?"

"Yes, you're right. I really wanted this to work. I wanted David and believed I needed him. I've always needed a man, especially for my son."

Suzanne had an excellent position as office manager of a large firm in town. While she made good money and could support herself and Tommy, she still admitted the need for a man in her life. During counseling she shared that that essentially was the way she had been brought up:

"Mom always told me that someday I'd meet 'Mr. Right' and that he would take care of me. My mother always deferred to my father. For example, if we were going out to dinner, she'd always say, 'Your father has worked hard all day—we'll go wherever Daddy takes us!'"

With her mother as a role model, Suzanne grew up being programmed to believe that unless she had a man, she was not complete. In all of her relationships with men, she had simply been "following her feelings," hoping that each one would turn out to be "Mr. Right" after all. To help Suzanne gain some perspective on how to tell the difference between just "following your feelings" and relating to a man with more cognitive common sense, I spent one of our sessions talking about a "mythical marvelous man." The conversation went something like this:

Dr. L.: What would happen if a man came into your place of business and struck up a conversation with you? He seems like a very nice guy and asks you out. What would you do?

Suzanne: Well, I'm not sure. If he were really nice, I'd probably be tempted to go out with him, but from what you've been telling me, that would be a little fast.

Dr. L.: Well, suppose you put him off but he came back and continued to impress you as a nice guy and kept asking for a date?

Suzanne: I'd probably go out with him.

Dr. L.: Suppose the two of you go out to dinner and he brings you home and wonders if he can come in for a few minutes?

Suzanne: Obviously you want me to say I wouldn't invite him in, that sex precludes intimacy, and I'd be stupid to risk going to bed with him on the first date.

Dr. L.: Okay, let's suppose he doesn't ask to come in. In fact, maybe he enjoys having a little fun and he asks you for your key, which probably makes you think, *Here we go again.* But instead, he just unlocks your door and hands it back and says he had a great time and he'll call you. Then he leaves without even trying for a kiss good night.

Suzanne: I'd begin to wonder if I had lost my touch, or if maybe this guy wasn't quite normal, if you know what I mean. . . .

Dr. L.: Well, as long as I'm describing a mythical man in this very fictional story, let's just take it down the road a little further. Suppose he suggests that he'll pick you up on a Saturday around 10:00 a.m., and you're to dress informally for a picnic. And he takes you up into the mountains and you have a great time sitting on the blanket, playing the portable tape player, enjoying the sun and the stream, eating and talking, and just having a good time. Then on the way home he suggests that you ought to do that again, but next time, why don't you bring Tommy?

Suzanne: Well, I'd just be thrilled to death. You know that.

Dr. L.: Okay, and suppose when you get to your front door he says, "Would it be all right if I give you a kiss?" How would you feel?

Suzanne: Oh, I would feel just wonderful. I'd think Mr. Right had walked into my life, and I'd feel I had fallen in

205

love . . . [and then, with a pained look on her face] where *is* this guy?

Dr. L.: Believe it or not, there are men out there who care enough about themselves to be able to care about someone else. Their actions are sincere, not manipulative. There are men who aren't living by the law of instant gratification and trying to "score" with every woman they can. I took you through this corny little story and described this mythical man to help you think about what it would be like to be with a person like this. Now, all you have to do is wait until he comes along.

Suzanne: That's easy for you to say. The man doesn't have to sit home waiting for the phone to ring. . . .

Dr. L.: I'm not discounting that, but you are attractive and out in the business community every day. You will have your share of male interest, but the point I'm making is that you don't have to be physically intimate with a man to be sure he hangs around. If he doesn't respect your feelings about waiting for physical intimacy, it's pretty obvious from your own bitter experience with David that such a man isn't worth having anyway.

Suzanne: Well, okay . . . but sometimes, Dr. Leman, you make it sound as if men are the only ones who enjoy sex. Women like sex too, and I'm one of them.

Dr. L.: I appreciate that and I'm not discounting that for a moment, Actually, studies show that women have a greater capacity to enjoy sex than men do. But what I'm trying to get at here is that what you're looking for is real emotional and personal *intimacy*, not just settling for the crumbs of being *his* sexual satisfaction. Until you can stop telling yourself the lie that you have to be physically intimate with a man or he will go away, you will continue to be taken advantage of by guys like David who may seem very nice, but their bottom line is still a desire to use you for their own ends. I would think you are tired of that.

206

Suzanne and I had several more sessions and conversations about the difference between becoming emotionally intimate with a man and just limiting the relationship to physical intimacy. I recall saying with a great deal of emphasis:

"Next time around, keep your mistakes with David in mind. You hardly *knew* him. He was a liar and a cheat. He could have been a bisexual or even a sadist . . . he could have been infected with herpes or AIDS. These are the realities today!"

Suzanne admitted the realities were there but that childhood training about needing a man was powerful and hard to erase. It was slow going to get her to see that she really didn't need a man unless he was the right kind.

One thing that really bothered her was the widely publicized survey by two Yale sociologists and a Harvard economist, which does not give the woman over thirty a lot of hope for ever getting married or remarried. According to the findings of the survey, only 20 percent of white, college-educated women over thirty can expect to marry. At age thirty-five the odds drop to 5 percent, and at forty, 1 percent.

Reports increasingly reveal an "epidemic" of single women over thirty appearing in the waiting rooms of counselors, psychologists, and psychotherapists across the country. They don't put their problem in terms of "wanting to get married," but sooner or later the hidden agenda comes out. Many women over thirty are beginning to panic. They come to counseling to find out why they haven't been able to develop a stable relationship with a man—in other words, marriage.

The problem is so widespread that one Los Angeles psychologist was quoted as saying, "I would suspect that the great majority of any psychotherapist's practice—maybe two-thirds of anybody's practice—is single women who have relationship problems."[4]

By the time Suzanne left counseling, she was buying into my theories and was dating a thirty-eight-year-old investment broker who almost fit the characteristics of the "mythical marvelous man" I described. Did they develop a serious relationship that led to marriage? To date I haven't heard, but that is not the point. I can only hope that counseling helped Suzanne grow enough to realize that a mature woman is complete and can see men as "just desserts," not as a main course that she can't live without. If a woman can't see a man as someone who can complement her own completeness, she is always in danger of being an hors d'oeuvre he enjoys for the moment—or possibly a few years—and then discards.

Sad to say, a vast majority of women have not reached this stage of completeness and maturity. Robin Norwood, author of *Women Who Love Too Much*, makes a good observation about the single woman: "Women who don't have a man think they'd be fine if they had one, and vice versa."[5] I counsel many single women who would like to be married because they need husbands. And I counsel many married women who'd like to be free of all the pain and frustration caused by dancing to the familiar "pleaser/controller waltz."

Some women manage this waltz quite well and come to terms with their controller husbands. But in too many cases, superpleasing women suffer in pain and depression with mates who are misogynists or addictive personalities of one kind or another.

A dangerous trap for many pleasers is the Martha Luther Complex, which I mentioned in earlier chapters. The metaphorical Martha Luther is fictitious, of course, and I get her name from Martin Luther, the well-known church reformer of the sixteenth century. The Martha Luther behavior pattern is very evident in many pleasing women who hook up with a man who has a "small drinking problem" or a "bit of a temper." Martha just knows she can smooth out these rough spots; just give her a little time and she'll change him to fit her image of Prince Charming.

From what I've heard in many counseling sessions, many Martha Luther pleasers wind up with Super Controllers who turn out to have serious drinking problems, explosive tempers, and numerous other hang-ups that make life miserable. For these Supersuffering Pleasers, "It can't get any worse than this." They are the subject of our next chapter.

9

Which Way Out
of Controller Swamp?

"Nice men are so boring. It could be worse;
he says he's sorry—afterward."

Jennifer's reddish-blonde hair and pouty look reminded
me of Hollywood star Bernadette Peters. Unfortunately,
her story reminded me of a stereotype Hollywood marriage
that had gone nowhere but downhill.

As Jennifer endured fifteen years with Al, she had four
boys while he had at least four affairs that she knew about.
In one case, she came home to find Al in bed with another woman while he was supposed to be caring for their
four-year-old son. But Jennifer never gave up. She hung
in there and even made excuses for Al, telling herself he
wouldn't wander if only she were a better wife and "more
of a woman" for him.

Was it another of Al's affairs that brought them in for counseling? No, the Supersuffering Pleaser had finally turned the tables. It was *her* affair that brought them in for counseling, with Al, a very macho type, bellowing like a bull about being betrayed.

Rats, Super Rats, and Ultra Rats

We'll use Jennifer and Al as a representative example of numerous case studies based on very real people who have sat in my office. Women like Jennifer represent the depressed and supersuffering women who occupy the bottom levels of the Pyramid of Pleasers introduced in chapter 1. Their husbands are what could be called "Super Punishing Controllers," or to put it in the vernacular used by women clients themselves, Rats, Super Rats, and even Ultra Rats!

Perhaps we need to pause and reflect just a moment on the word *rat*. My experience with men and women over the years shows it is seldom true that any person is "all rat." The husband who might be the Super Punishing Controller (Super Rat) doesn't wake up each morning and say, "Ah! Another day to torture and abuse my wife physically, mentally, and emotionally! I guess I'd better get right to it!"

In fact, at work he might be known as the benevolent employer or manager—a kind and gentle man who treats his staff with understanding and empathy. But at home he is a controller. He is at the center of his world. Everything and everyone revolves around him, and he uses everything an d everyone—especially his wife—to gratify his desires and needs.

In extreme cases, he may be labeled a misogynist, the term used by Susan Forward and Joan Torres in their excellent best-selling work, *Men Who Hate Women and the*

Women Who Love Them. According to Dr. Forward, who was married to such a man, this kind of husband seems to be capable of loving deeply, intensely, and with much sexual passion, but in fact, he does everything he can to destroy the woman he says he loves so much.[1]

The misogynist has the overwhelming need to control, and his chief weapons are words and moods. He may physically abuse his wife, but he is far more likely to specialize in psychological battery, which can be just as destructive as physical blows, if not more so. If you suspect you are getting "misogynized," here are some key signs:

He believes it is his right to control you and in trying to please him you may have decided to give up activities or people you felt were important just to keep life smooth.

He puts you down and either "blows his top" or turns to ice when you disappoint him. You do a lot of "walking on eggs," always trying to think of the right thing to do or say, so he won't be upset.

He can be a Jekyll-and-Hyde type—charming and even affectionate one moment and mean and unbelievably abusive the next. This may be especially true if he is a user of alcohol or drugs. When you're not walking on eggs you're on pins and needles—confused, scared, feeling inadequate and no good.

In one area, however, you feel no uncertainty or confusion. There is never any doubt about who is always to blame for whatever has gone wrong, has seemed to go wrong, or what might go wrong. *You* are, period.

He may be very jealous and possessive, not wanting you to get out much, always wanting you at home and handy to do his bidding. One way he might show his possessiveness is to be a great gift giver. But please remember there is no free lunch. When a woman puts high value on security, a controller can keep her nicely in line with a lot of expensive gifts. The wealthy or well-to-do controller uses gifts to keep the balance of power in his favor. It also fuels the pleaser's desire to defend him and to justify her situation.

I've talked to many such women in counseling and eventually the truth about his "gift giving" comes out. The husband does not let his wife spend much money at her own discretion, but he lavishes gifts on her—"those little things she's always wanted." A critical point, however, is that he is always in control, spending the money *as he sees fit*.

Martha Luther Is Often in the Helping Professions

This same kind of supercontrolling rat is described in Robin Norwood's excellent book, *Women Who Love Too Much*, which has also struck a chord with thousands of female readers across the nation. Rather than centering on misogynists, Dr. Norwood discusses the woman who is attracted to the kind of man who is unpredictable, immature, moody, distant, and quite possibly addicted to alcohol or other drugs. She desperately tries to reform, fix, help, or improve him in every way she can.[2]

This pleasing woman suffers from what I have already labeled the Martha Luther complex. She is often found in helping professions such as nursing or teaching. She might be a counselor or a therapist. But whatever her calling, she is drawn to the needy, hurting man because she "understands him." And in helping him she finds the love and security that was missing in her own life, particularly while growing up.

This superpleasing woman who loves too much is an expert at finding the loser with the broken wing. And the loser spots her with equal skill and intuition. It is almost as if she has a red cross or perhaps the words *Wounded Wing Society* tattooed on her heart, and only the needy loser has the Clark Kent eyes that enable him to see the label.

They make a perfect match. The more emotionally unavailable, irresponsible, or flaky he appears, the better she likes it. And the more helping, caring, and understanding she is, the better he likes it. He knows instinctively, "Here's the woman who will take care of me," just like guess who? Good ol' Mom!

If you are this kind of woman, it is quite likely you will go to extreme lengths to make the relationship work. Because you are a natural fixer, you are willing to carry far more than 50 percent of the load. You take most of the responsibility to keep everything smooth and most of the blame when things get bumpy. You may also carry a lot of guilt for "not being a better wife."

Ironically, you may sincerely believe you have fairly high self-esteem. You may be coming apart on the inside, but on the outside you're saying, "Look at me. I'm capable, successful—I'll match my schedule with anyone!" What you may not be willing to admit to yourself is that you are working hard to prove your worth and value, and you mask your lack of self-esteem with overachieving and ultra busyness. You gather trophies, degrees, and labels to reassure yourself, "I'm okay."

Another approach the pleaser may take to shoring up her self-esteem is having lots of friends. She may be popular, known for being a lot of fun (or very generous and giving), but it is all a front. What she really yearns for is that attention, respect, and love from the man in her life.

Another distinctive characteristic of the Martha Luther pleaser is that she is efficient, hardworking, and helpful in order to keep her husband at bay. Her basic motivation is fear. She does not want to be controlled or overwhelmed, so she becomes a "defensive controller" who controls her husband in helpful ways in order to protect herself and her own security. She is, in reality, still a pleaser at heart. The true controller, on the other hand, is one who loves to take charge, dominate, manipulate, and pull the strings to meet personal needs and goals. The true controller is on the offensive, not the defensive.

Pleasing and Discouragement Can Be Unhappy Bedfellows

Two words that fit the Depressed or Supersuffering Pleaser are *hurt* and *discouraged*. I have found that the lower a woman lands on the Pyramid of Pleasers, the more discouraged she is (see p. 219).

At the top of the pyramid we have the Positive Pleaser, who has a great deal of hope and very little discouragement. Hers is a balanced life and, while she enjoys pleasing others, she gets the respect, love, and support she needs in return, especially from her husband.

Coming down the pyramid one notch we have the Mildly Discouraged Pleaser, who is just that. She feels just a bit under it all, with a vague feeling that it would be nice to get a little more respect, a little more positive feedback. She also would like to be able to handle situations better and be able to say no with more conviction and less guilt.

In the center of the pyramid we have the Played-Out Pleaser, who may be feeling quite discouraged. The chief source of her discouragement is exhaustion. She is just plain tired—tired of running, doing, feeling trapped. She feels like a cabby and her minivan isn't even yellow!

Ironically, the Played-Out Pleaser is her own worst enemy and the key source of her own troubles. She does all this running, doing, and pleasing because she "knows" that if she doesn't people won't like her, accept her, or love her.

As we near the bottom of the pyramid, we have the Depressed Pleaser, who has many of the characteristics named immediately above. Because she is trying to fill a void that started way back in her childhood, she is almost always hooked up with a man who causes her pain. Ironically, this is the only kind of man to whom she can relate. She wants to fix him, help him, please him, and she just knows that someday he might change. But it isn't working—he has turned out to be a drinker, addicted to drugs, or perhaps addicted to work or other women. She loves him—too much—and is paying a terrible price.

At the bottom of the pyramid is the Supersuffering Pleaser, who is in the hands of the cruelest kind of controller. We can give him all kinds of labels: misogynist, Rat, Super Rat, or Ultra Rat. He is basically an extremely immature, selfish, insecure individual who has placed himself at the center of his universe and is using his wife as an emotional punching bag, servant, and geisha girl.

For the Supersuffering Pleaser, discouragement, hurt, and hopelessness can reach 100 percent. She may often gain weight and start to care very little about her grooming and the way her house looks. She may say, "I never thought I'd let myself go like this."

Which Way Out of the Swamp?

To begin finding your way out of Controller Swamp, you need to take several simple but extremely important steps.

Decide to Act

Sounds easy enough, you're probably thinking. *And just what kind of action would you like me to take?*

I agree that "deciding to act" sounds simplistic, but it is always the simple things that are extremely difficult. Taking action is often difficult for the pleasing personality, who has always waited for others to make the first move. That's why pleasers wind up in the hands of controllers.

The key is not to try changing your situation overnight. Frankly, if you are married to a Super Punishing Controller (i.e., Rat or worse), it may take months to make measurable progress. But you must start somewhere.

Be encouraged. Just by reading this book you have made an important start. The next step may call for a visit to a competent psychologist, or perhaps a marriage and family counselor. Shop around. Look for a psychologist or counselor who really values the institution of marriage. Today too many counselors and therapists believe in "disposable marriages." A marriage is not a box of Pampers or a Happy Birthday tablecloth that lasts until the party's over and then is tossed out. Don't slip back into your pleasing ways and "stick it out" with a therapist who makes you uncomfortable.

My personal bias is toward the kind of counselor who "wants to get rid of you." In other words, he or she believes in short-term therapy. While some cases will take quite a bit longer than others, I believe in therapy that usually lasts less than a year and often no more than four to six months.

I tell my clients I am not trying to be a "bargain center" psychologist; I simply work on the premise that all of us have learned to be the way we are and we can unlearn some of that behavior. When I deal with a client on a short-term basis, that is encouraging to the client in and of itself. When

0 full of hope and
encouragement

5

25

75

95

100

Positive Pleaser Good balance between pleasing nature and receiving the respect, support, and love she wants and needs.

Mildly Discouraged Pleaser Pluses usually outweigh the minuses, but she knows life could be a great deal better if she knew how to get the world to show her a little more respect.

Played-Out (Exhausted) Pleaser Making a go of life, but feeling stressed out, tired, and fatigued. She can't say no, and always has to do the giving in any relationship.

Depressed Pleaser Hurt, miserable, and unhappy, often connected to a loser or womanizer, whom she feels she has to care for and help. (Occupationally, the Depressed Pleaser is often a nurse or other professional care giver.) May need professional help.

Supersuffering Pleaser In real pain, probably has relationship with a misogynist, needs professional help.

Totally Discouraged
As a woman goes deeper and deeper into pleasing, she becomes more and more discouraged and feeling hopeless.

she knows I don't plan to see her indefinitely, she can tell herself, *The counselor really thinks I have potential to change. He thinks I can handle this.*

And so once we identify the problem and set up a practical game plan for changing behavior, I "push the client out of the nest." I tell her, "You go on back out there and try flying on your own. If you get stuck or crash, call back and we'll give you some additional help."

But perhaps you feel you aren't ready to try a counselor or psychologist just yet. Then I suggest that you at least stop and take stock. Part of your initial decision to seek change and improvement in your life is realizing you can't change him; *you can only change yourself.* You have to come to that place where you are willing to say, "I can't live like this anymore. I must do something differently."

Jennifer Went Shopping for Her Own Affair

The trick is to do something constructive and positive, not destructive, negative, or so confrontational that it causes such an explosion there is nothing left to work with. In Jennifer's case, she chose a destructive approach to her plight with Al, who had four affairs while she was having four children. Jennifer strongly suspected there were many other affairs but could point to only four she really knew about.

Al was a powerful controller who believed his life-style could be as carefree as he wanted it to be. He actually thought affairs were his prerogative, but when Jennifer had one he was outraged.

When Jennifer decided to make her move, she didn't run to a singles bar and grab the first interested man for a one-night stand. She actually "shopped" for a suitable partner and found him at work. Their friendship quickly blossomed into a heavy affair that went on for several months.

When Al found out (as Jennifer made sure he would), he was baffled and outraged. How could his sweet little wife do such a terrible thing?

Of course, Jennifer's tit-for-tat solution to her problem was no solution at all. Affairs are always destructive, and all you can learn from them is what is wrong with the marriage.

"And what *did* you learn?" I asked Jennifer as she sat with me in my office. "What made this affair with Larry so fulfilling?"

"Well, it was fun—and exciting. I wasn't just sitting around at home wondering who Al was taking to bed next."

"Was there a revenge factor—did you feel you were paying Al back?"

"I suppose so, especially at first. But then it turned into something really nice in one sense. Larry was nonjudgmental, interesting, and he *listened* to me. He respected what I said. We talked a lot."

Jennifer's glowing description of Larry's ability to be nonjudgmental and a good communicator left me with little doubt about what was wrong with her marriage to Al. There was no communication, but there was plenty of criticism. As for sex, Jennifer is one of many women who have told me in therapy that sex was a minimal part of an affair. She and Larry seldom had sex, but when they did it was very good because she felt he really loved and cherished her.

But while the affair with Larry had its plus features, the minus side was overwhelming. By the time Jennifer decided to start therapy, guilt and depression had reduced her to an emotional basket case. In our first sessions she wept periodically as we developed a mini life-style on her that included a father who was a strict disciplinarian, who seldom showed any physical affection, and who criticized Jennifer often. When things didn't go his way, he would pout or turn to ice. And, according to the same old "broken record pattern," Jennifer married Al, who was very demanding and possessive. Al was long on criticism and short on encouragement and compliments.

Jennifer learned to keep her opinions to herself around her husband and to walk softly at all times. She never felt she could be herself and was always careful not to get Al upset. Meanwhile, *she* was the one who had major cause to be upset, but through each of Al's affairs she had bitten the bullet and explained it by saying, "That's the way men are!"

My sessions with Al revealed a man who was an extreme chauvinist but not really an Ultra Rat or misogynist. Al had grown up in a home where his father had ruled with an iron hand and treated his wife like a puppy dog. Al learned from watching his dad that women are for a man's pleasure and convenience, that they should keep their place, and that they should always meet the man's needs.

At 5'10" tall and 170 pounds, Al was the typical macho athlete who had lettered in high school but hadn't been big enough for a college scholarship. He had settled for intramurals while getting a degree in business administration. After marrying Jennifer and settling down in his job as a junior account executive with an aerospace firm, he continued playing city league basketball and softball throughout the year. Of course, he wanted Jennifer at all his games, cheering for him and making him feel like the superjock he thought he was.

My talks with Al also revealed an ironic twist. While he saw little wrong with being a wandering womanizer, he had a hard time trusting Jennifer! He would call her at work to be sure she was there. He often imagined she was being unfaithful to him.

The psychological term for suspecting or accusing others of doing the very thing you are guilty of is *projection*, and Al was a classic example. Because he was running around with other women, he excused his guilt by thinking Jennifer was undoubtedly doing the same thing.

While Jennifer's affair was a traumatic shock to the marriage, she did get Al's attention and sent him a clear message:

"I won't stand for this anymore. I want a new arrangement and a better life."

I spent many sessions trying to establish communication between Jennifer and Al. I had them do a bit of "reflecting," which simply means one person (the sender) talks while the other (the receiver) listens and then reflects or feeds back what he or she believes was said. If the sender feels misunderstood, he or she has the chance to clarify or restate feelings more specifically.

On Al's side, I had to deal with a lot of hurt and anger. He simply couldn't believe Jennifer would betray him, and he kept throwing her affair with Larry in her face at every opportunity. You may be wondering how he would have the gall to do this after having had four affairs of his own, but this only underscores Al's immature thinking and perspective. In the early stages of therapy, he just couldn't see that his affairs had hurt Jennifer as much or more than her single affair had hurt him. To Al, it was "different—all men chase around a little . . . it doesn't mean anything . . . they still love their families. . . ."

Al's incredibly immature attitude reminded me of another male client who once told me, "Hey, Doc, I've been a good husband. In fourteen years of marriage, I've had only eight other women."

As for Jennifer, I worked hard at helping her raise her self-image and analyze her response to Al's controlling ways. Early in counseling, I gave Jennifer a second important principle for getting out of her swamp of discouragement.

Make Your Needs Important, Too

I know many pleasers will think this advice sounds selfish, but hear me out. For a pleaser trapped in Controller

Swamp, it is definitely the right move. By making your needs as important as your husband's and those of the rest of your family, you will not turn into a selfish monster. Instead, it will put more balance and equality into your marriage and other relationships. In Jennifer's case, she had never set any limits for Al and, selfish controller that he was, he had simply taken more and more for granted and more and more advantage.

"I'm not excusing Al's philandering for a moment," I told Jennifer, "but when you didn't set any limits, you taught your husband he could walk all over you and he did just that."

"What do you mean limits—what kind of limits?"

"Well, for one thing, you can tell Al that you simply can't get to all of his ball games. With a full-time job and four boys to raise, it's my guess you have your hands full. They probably have games of their own. By the way, is Al taking any interest in the kids?"

"The two older boys are in Little League, but Al hasn't had time to see them play much. He's one of the best pitchers on his softball team and they play two or three nights a week."

"Then it's time for Al to do some choosing. It sounds as if he's still working out some adolescent fantasies about being an athlete. It has come down to softball or you and the children. The other thing that goes with setting limits is speaking up. Start telling Al how you feel about things. Start using more phrases such as 'I'm going to . . . ,' 'I believe it would be fair if . . . ,' 'I want you to take me more seriously about. . . .' The point is, it's okay to say, 'I want.'"

That one was hard for Jennifer to swallow. A super pleaser to the core, she had always felt that putting her needs, desires, and wants first was selfish—even sinful. It took her a while to see that the person with healthy self-esteem can express her wants and needs without being selfish or greedy. In fact, to be unable or unwilling to express one's wants and needs is as bad as being greedy and grasping. How can husband and wife ever establish healthy communication if they can't share what is on their minds?

Jennifer also had trouble with what I call the "please read my mind" syndrome. Many, if not most, wives do not even realize it, but they want their husbands to be able to read their minds. Time and again, women have said to me in different ways, "If he really loved me, he'd *know* what I want and need." Women want their husbands to anticipate their needs and meet those needs *without being asked.* Ideally, this is what is psychologically and emotionally fulfilling for a woman.

What I had to point out to Jennifer was that she was not working with the ideal situation just yet. When she did start telling Al what she wanted and he did it, she had to be careful not to say to herself, *Yes, he did it, but only because I asked him to and not because he really wanted to!*

Of course he would do it because she asked him to! That was to be part of the training process. After all, she had to start somewhere to escape her Swamp of Discouragement.

"And something else you must do, when Al tries to please you after you speak up, is to give him some positive reinforcement and say something like, 'I see you're really making an effort and that pleases me. It makes me feel special.'"

Al and Jennifer made slow progress but fortunately—and quite surprisingly, after Jennifer's affair—they were both willing to stick with therapy and try to repair their marriage. When confronted with putting his own recreation ahead of his sons', Al bristled at first but eventually found

225

time to attend more Little League games. He even started talking about "maybe coaching next year."

As Jennifer began ever so timidly to express her feelings and wants, Al started to realize that he was not the center of the universe. He became less judgmental and critical and began to understand that he had harbored some very negative, even sick, ideas about women.

Forgiveness is a lovely word, and an even lovelier thought, but it is a long process. As the pain eased for both of them, Al and Jennifer were able to forgive each other and start building a relationship in which they began to value one another. They started to realize what the two of them could do together to cope with life's pressures and stress.

Most people are acquainted with the Old Testament passage that speaks of a man cleaving to his wife and their becoming "one flesh."[3] There is much to be said for two becoming one in marriage, if the "one" is a team made up of two complete and mature persons who both bring strengths and gifts to the union.

I fear that in too many cases men believe "two becoming one" means a woman gives up her own selfhood in some way, in order to "be completed" by the man she married. But as Sonya Friedman says in *Men Are Just Desserts*, this warped understanding can only overshadow the true *oneness* "which has to do with the importance of personal growth within a marriage by two people who, as separate individuals, reach for a common goal."[4]

Jennifer and Al are going to struggle for quite a while, but I am convinced they will make it. During their course of therapy, they attended a Marriage Encounter weekend, where they learned some excellent techniques for communicating and realized that they had been missing out on a powerful resource to draw from: the spiritual side of life. They picked a church both of them were comfortable with, and slowly began to experience a oneness that had been missing in their fifteen years of marriage.

Attending church was particularly difficult for Al, who was convinced that churches were for hypocrites. Jennifer had tried to take her children to church on a hit-and-miss basis, but without Al's support it had been mostly miss. When the two of them joined together in building the spiritual dimension of their family, the results were pleasantly surprising to both of them. Al actually became the spiritual leader of his family, much to Jennifer's delight.

Before we move on, I want to put two strong qualifications on this case study:

1. It was a happy, storybook type of ending that may arouse cynical feelings of disbelief on the part of some readers. They know of women whose affairs didn't turn out this well at all. I am happy to report that this case really did turn out just the way it is described. I share the good news and happy ending to stress that there is hope. People can change their behavior and find a way out of the Swamp of Discouragement and Despair.

2. More important, I do not share this story to excuse or glamorize affairs in any way. The last thing I want to do is suggest that the best way for a Supersuffering Pleaser to get a Super Punishing Controller's attention is to have an affair. A misleading bit of "talk show psychology" that seems to drift around the airwaves these days is that if a woman wants to get her wandering husband's attention, she should have a counteraffair just to put him in his place.

I do not advocate affairs in any form. In fact, the thought makes me shudder because in most cases the damage is irreparable. Al and Jennifer were able to find a therapist and patch things up, but frankly, they were lucky. It is my

227

guess that less than one out of ten, possibly one out of fifty, marriages survive affairs. In most cases, the wounds are so deep, there is very little for a therapist to try to save.

Yet, it can happen—especially if the wife is strong enough to use cognitive self-discipline when she would prefer to use a gun or perhaps a horsewhip. I say, "Bravo!" to the woman who can respond to her husband's affair as did one betrayed wife who discovered his philandering after a nineteen-year marriage. Instead of calling her lawyer, she sat down and asked herself some hard questions:

- Would the children benefit emotionally and financially from a divorce? (No. Their lives would be disrupted. They would miss their father a great deal.)
- Would my career benefit from a divorce? (No. My job requires total concentration, 40–50 hours a week.)
- Would my husband's family—elderly parents, close siblings—benefit from a divorce? (No. It would kill his mother. She believes him to be the perfect son, husband, and father.)
- Do I want to change my life-style? (No.)
- What is the bottom line regarding my feelings? Can I live with and recover from wounded pride? (Yes.)

The wife and her husband talked at length and made a two-way pact: He would end the affair and never have another; she would never mention his affair or the woman again.

Now it is five years later and both have lived up to the agreement. They never bring up the past, and he is a better husband than before: "more caring, more compassionate and sexier." As for her "pride," she has more self-esteem than ever because she knows she did the right thing. She can face and conquer anything that life might throw at her.[5]

I know from my counseling experiences that pleasers *can* handle life with controllers—*if they are really willing to make some changes*. In the following chapter I want you to meet several more pleasers and learn additional strategies for escaping Controller Swamp once and for all.

10

Taming the Alligator,
Draining the Swamp

"But Dr. Leman, what can I do? I don't believe in divorce."

In chapter 9, we covered some obvious first steps for any super pleaser who is looking for a way out of the Swamp of Discouragement, where she is barely able to keep treading water in a relationship with a Super Controller husband:

First you must decide to act, to change things.

Then you must start making your needs important, too.

These first steps are terribly simple and basic, but if the Supersuffering Pleaser doesn't have the conviction to follow through, she is doomed to disappointment and will sink even deeper into the swamp.

Many clients tell me, "I'll try to change, Doctor Leman."

I reply, "*Trying* won't cut it. You must say 'I will' and mean it. And then you must start to behave differently and never look back. You can keep going to friends, pastors, counselors, and therapists all your life and complain, cry, get sympathy and more advice, but *nothing will change until you do*."

If you are serious about using cognitive self-discipline to change your behavior, here are three additional steps you can take to start draining your Swamp of Discouragement and taming that alligator you mistook for a prince back when you got married:

- Stop denying reality.
- Don't buy into his behavior.
- Expect and overcome opposition.

We'll look first at the crucial need to stop denying reality. As you work at change and making your needs important, you must have a clear perspective. What is the situation? What are the issues? What are both of you up against? You may be trying to work on the problem without correctly identifying what the *real* problem is. A marriage with problems is often like a logjam. If you can locate the key log and loosen it, the entire jam will let go.

The Case of the Revolving-Door Husband

Norene was forty-five, mother of Lori, nineteen, who was soon to leave for college, and Lance, sixteen, who didn't seem to be going anywhere in particular. Norene was married to Barney, forty-nine, who had prematurely gray hair and stood two inches shorter than his wife.

Norene came from an ultra-authoritarian home. She never said much except, "Yes ma'am" and "No sir." She did as she was told. She was a very cooperative, pleasing child—until she grew up and had the chance to rebel. At age twenty she met Barney and married him to get out of the house, which she considered the frying pan. Unfortunately, she jumped right into the fire and spent twenty-five years of hell on earth with a man who had a habit of moving out of the house, staying with other women, and eventually returning to his wife.

How many times had Barney done his revolving-door act? If my profession convinces me of anything, it is that truth *is* much stranger and harder to believe than fiction. In twenty-five years, Barney had moved out and back in *over thirty times.*

Sixteen-year-old Lance had watched Dad walk all over Mom and was following in his controlling footsteps. He told Norene off, swore at her, and never cleaned up his room because, of course, she would come along later and do it.

For his sixteenth birthday, Lance insisted on getting a motorcycle. Norene was in counseling by that time and I advised, "Absolutely no motorcycle." But any woman who would allow a husband to come back time and again after deserting her and sleeping with other women was no match for an insistent teenager. Besides, he was failing in school and Norene hoped a new motorcycle would inspire him to greater academic heights.

Lance got his motorcycle and six days later was involved in an accident with a fifteen-year-old girl on a bicycle. The girl went to the hospital and her parents wanted to go to court. Norene, a super pleaser whose low self-esteem and high guilt factor had always kept her trying to appease Barney and Lance, was ready to go to a desert island—anywhere to get away from the zoo she had to call her life.

Somehow Norene got through those weeks following the accident. Fortunately, the girl Lance hit made a good recovery and her parents were willing to settle out of court with Norene's insurance company. Part of the price included Lance's "right to wheels" because his driving record now made insurance premiums prohibitive. Norene was a confused mixture of rage, frustration, and guilt, but she was ready and willing to do something to change what had become intolerable. During counseling I stressed still another basic premise for Supersuffering Pleasers who want to take positive action toward a better life: *Stop believing the lies you have been telling yourself for years. Don't be a guilt sponge who soaks up blame and criticism from the controllers in your life.*

Norene had all kinds of guilt that she had gathered from listening to her authoritarian parents criticize and lay down the law. Her guilt escalated when she married Barney against their wishes and spent twenty-five years in a sick, downward spiral of being periodically deserted and betrayed by a controlling, loser husband who did not want to change.

"Norene," I said, "I'd like to see you try using what I call cognitive self-discipline to start thinking about a few things. Everyone's behavior is a choice. We really don't have to do anything; we choose to do what we do. You are choosing to believe a lot of lies that started to crop up back when you were a little girl. You tell yourself that you're no good, that there's something wrong with you, and that you deserve this kind of life. All this is a negative habit pattern, but you can change it if you choose to do so. The next time your little girl of the past starts telling you all those lies, learn to call time-out. Tell yourself, *I am an adult . . . my little girl from the past is not running my life . . . I am in control . . . I am responsible for me.*"

Norene tried to put my advice into action but had little success at first. I told her, "You must realize this is a new skill you are trying to develop. You need practice—not to be perfect, but to improve."

Barney Finally Made One Exit Too Many

Despite being trapped in a marriage that could have been a solid candidate for a new TV series called *In Search of the Strange and Bizarre*, Norene had hung in there. Somehow she lasted twenty-five years with Barney, who was a strange combination of weak little boy who needed mothering (he actually called Norene "Mother"), and a Super Punishing Controller who would hold her down to satisfy his sexual urges, leaving her feeling raped and used. In twenty-five years, Norene had never experienced any pleasurable feelings of orgasm.

"Barney didn't make love to me," she said with a bitter smile. "He just satisfied himself, rolled over, and went to sleep."

When I got into Barney's background it was not too hard to see where he had learned his attitudes toward women. His parents had been killed in an auto accident and he had been reared by his grandparents on a farm in the Midwest. The key person in his life was his grandfather, a powerful, dominating figure who walked all over Barney's doting grandmother. Barney grew up getting daily lessons that told him it was a man's prerogative to do whatever he wanted with and to the woman in his life.

At the same time, Barney had many weak spots. He needed a woman to mother him the way Grandma had done. When he met Norene he sensed that she was the one. They married and began their strange pleaser/controller dance.

When life got too tense for Barney, his solution was to leave, often for days, even for weeks at a time. On many occasions he failed to show up for work and was fired. Through the years he had many jobs—and any number of women, to whom he would run when he "left" Norene.

But Barney never left for good. He always returned and Norene would continue mothering him. She was a classic example of Martha Luther, always taking over, always trying to reform and "help" Barney cut down on his drinking, get to his job, get another job. Of course, Norene had always had to work full-time herself to be sure there was money for basics when Barney went into his "run away from home" act.

A few months after Norene began therapy and started making progress, her situation took a turn I did not anticipate. Anytime I counsel a troubled marriage, my first goal is to save that marriage and build it into the strong kind of union that Jennifer and Al managed to create out of their chaos. But in this case, Barney's revolving-door life-style proved to be too much.

After taking part in a few counseling sessions, Barney left again and stayed away for almost three months. During that time, Norene met a man at church, where she played the piano for an adult class. Wally started attending the class and kept noticing this woman who seemed unattached. They struck up a friendship, and for the first time in years

Norene had a glimmer of realization that she could be attractive to a man who would treat her nicely.

To say she had an affair with Wally would be totally inaccurate. To my surprise, in whirlwind fashion she decided to marry Wally and migrate north to the upper Midwest, where she began building a new and truly happy life.

I get at least one letter a year from Norene in which she gives me all of her news, most of which is good and positive. Lance chose to stay with his father, while his sister, Lori, decided to live with Norene and Wally until finishing college. Her second marriage has been everything her first marriage was not.

One thing Norene took plenty of time to do before marrying Wally was to learn about his relationships to the women in his life. She was able to visit with his two older sisters, and found a warm relationship existing between them and their brother. When Norene casually asked them about their mother, who was deceased, the sisters told her that Wally had always been close to her as well.

Something I tell any woman who is contemplating marriage or remarriage is to take a hard look at the family you are marrying into. Essentially, you are marrying all the problems, strengths, and blessings in that family. What you see is what you get—the choice is yours.

For twenty-five years Norene had denied reality and stayed in what was really a "nonmarriage" to a man who was half controlling monster and half helpless little boy. When Norene finally faced reality, she was able to salvage her self-esteem and build a new life.

Let me stress again that when I counsel the partners in a troubled marriage, my goal is to save the marriage and build it into a strong union. But the fact is, sometimes a marriage can't be saved. Barney had no interest in growing up and treating Norene the way she deserved to be treated.

In the next case, Louise faced an even more serious problem than Norene's. By ignoring reality, she put herself in mortal danger.

For Louise, Time Was Running Out

At thirty-nine, Louise was tall and had once been attractive. Now she was haggard and hollow-eyed. Her hair hung in straggly bunches. Her hands shook and her clothes had a thrown-on look that suggested she had much more on her mind than appearance.

She did. Her husband, Michael, forty-one, was stocky, hard driving—and hard drinking. When the pressures of his vice-president's job with a large supermarket chain became heavy, he drank far too much. When drunk, which was almost every weekend, he would say unbelievably vulgar and derogatory things to Louise. On several occasions he had ripped off her clothes, bounced her off the wall, and raped her. The next morning he could not remember a thing.

But Louise remembered—every word, every blow. When she would tell Michael what had happened, he would be the picture of remorse. He couldn't believe he had done such things. He would beg her forgiveness, hold her close, kiss her, promising it would never happen again. And so Louise would forgive . . . and hope . . . and live in fear . . . until it did happen again.

Louise had come to see me because the pain and fear had reached desperate, life-threatening levels. Michael's drunken rages and incredible verbal abuse, during which he made profuse use of words such as *slob*, *stupid slut*, *ugly*, *wrinkled*, and *sagging*, had become weekly occurrences.

Why did Louise take this kind of treatment? Her mini life-style revealed what popular psychological jargon calls a "dysfunctional home." That is, she was raised in a cross between a zoo and a combat zone. One reason she had stuck it out with Michael was that she knew from experience how to roll with his verbal and sometimes physical punches.

Her father had been the worst kind of tyrant. When Louise described him, she said, "My father didn't give a hoot about Mother or any of us. I tried to please him—I tried so hard—but terrible things went on that I have trouble even remembering now. I got beatings and whippings from my father for no reason. So did my sister and my mother. My sister and I would just lie there in bed and pull the covers up over our heads and press the pillows to our ears to block out the screaming, yelling, and even the breaking of glass. We would pretend to be asleep if he walked into our room."

Louise was still another example of a little girl who grew up vowing to never marry someone like her father, only to discover that she had done just that. Michael had been so sexy and smooth on those first dates. Louise could practically feel the electricity that seemed to pass between them. The honeymoon lasted about a year. Then Michael's frequent drinking, which Louise tried to minimize with weak jokes, became alarmingly heavy. When Michael started needing a drink the first thing in the morning and periodically throughout the day. Louise realized she had married an alcoholic.

All her life she had hoped and prayed for a marriage that would be relatively stress free. Now she found herself in more stress than ever with a man capable of saying and doing almost anything when he drank, which was most of the time. Louise wasn't just walking on eggs; she was wading knee-deep in omelette batter.

"You remind me of a sign on the wall at my dentist's office," I told her. "That sign says, THE FIVE MOST DANGEROUS WORDS IN THE ENGLISH LANGUAGE ARE, 'MAYBE IT WILL GO AWAY.' But this *isn't* going to go away. You are in serious trouble—real danger. You've been sweeping it all under the rug, hoping that somehow Michael might change. You found Michael exciting at first. A nice, stable man who never touched a drop probably would have been dull and uninteresting. But now you realize it's gone too far and you're hoping someone or something will rescue you. Well, no one is riding to the rescue in this one. And nothing will change unless you do. You have taken the first step by coming to see me, but that's just a bare start. We haven't got a lot of time to let you go on with this pain. Michael could easily maim or kill you. You must move out, now. Then confront him about his drinking. Tell him he either gets help or you're gone for good."

Louise was frightened enough to take my advice and move out immediately. She realized that by putting up with Michael's unbelievable abuse, she was solving nothing. She was being his enabler, who allowed him to pursue his alcoholism and sick life-style.

Moving out definitely got Michael's attention. He agreed to go into an alcoholic rehabilitation program and Louise joined Al-Anon. They are both still trying to piece together the shambles of their lives and their marriage.

To stop denying reality is an extremely important step. And it leads naturally into the next basic strategy that can help you drain your Swamp of Discouragement and turn that controlling alligator into at least a harmless frog—or with luck, a handsome prince. But he won't change unless you do, and part of your change is to *stop buying into his controlling behavior.*

Barbara Thought Dean's Silence Was All Her Fault

Barbara, thirty-five, married for a third time, was confident in all areas of life except with men. Her current husband, Dean, was a black-and-white thinker, insensitive, introspective, and silent most of the time. He would usually tune Barbara out, but he loved to play chess, go fishing, and drink, not necessarily in that order. When the booze flowed, so did the insults. He blamed Barbara for everything—his lousy job at the car-rental agency, poor luck fishing, losing chess games, you name it.

Barbara's first husband had been a teenage mistake. Her second had been eleven years older, a man who forced her to abort his child. And now she had Dean. Her batting average was zero for three and she came to me feeling "insecure and unloved." In her mini life-style workup, Barbara chose to describe her mother, "because it was easier."

Barbara's mother had been a super pleaser, motivated by guilt. She didn't have a very good relationship with her husband, but she had been very supportive of her children.

"Mom was always very understanding," Barbara recalled, "very giving, really. I guess she would be called permissive today."

"How about your father?"

"Well, he was strict, not affectionate at all. He didn't spend a lot of time with us. I grew up trying to be like my mother—very giving, not wanting to hurt anyone. In fact, I used to let my younger brother and little sister beat me up, even though I was much bigger and stronger. I guess you'd have to say I'm a very passive person deep inside."

For all of her passivity, Barbara had turned out much like Clarissa, the "powerful jellyfish" discussed in chapter 5. Clarissa, you may recall, was respected at work but scared to death when she went home to her husband, Jim.

Barbara was a real estate broker who had led sales for her agency over the past two years. At work, when she talked she was "Emily F. Hutton," and everybody listened. But when she got home and tried to say something to Dean, he usually didn't even give her the courtesy of a response, unless he wanted to complain or criticize.

Barbara admitted that she liked being in control of things at work. In her job, she was successful, able to please people and gain their approval. But at home, the passive little pleasing girl from the past was dominated by an unloving husband, because she would always buy into his controlling behavior. When he was silent, she did everything she could to get him to talk. When he was critical, she was apologetic, placating, and sure it was all her fault.

Barbara had always managed to find men who didn't really love her, but in one sense she acquired this "skill" from her permissive mother just as much as from her unaffectionate, distant father.

"Your mother always ran interference for you," I tried to explain. "She showed you how to accept lousy treatment from a man and what to expect from a man, which was not much. Your mother was long-suffering with your father, and to compensate she was overpermissive with you and your brother and sister because she felt guilty and to blame for not having a happier family. You knew you could always run to Mom for comfort and support, and she played the permissive role to keep your love. But she actually robbed you of psychological muscles you would need later in life."

Barbara's troubles with Dean did not include adultery. He wasn't running around with other women, but he was emotionally oblivious, totally wrapped up in his own little world, which was dominated by chess games and fishing trips. In addition, he was an alcoholic, but when Barbara expressed concern about his drinking, he would heatedly deny that he couldn't stop anytime he wanted to.

Another part of Barbara's workup revealed that every man in her life, those she had dated from age fourteen up, had left her. That is, the boys and later the men always broke off the relationships with her; she never broke off with them. For all of her passivity, Barbara had a tenacious, badgerlike streak. She would never give up on a man; he always gave up on her. After the mistake of a teenage marriage fresh out of high school that lasted only a few months, Barbara waited until age twenty-three to find a man eleven years her senior. Why pick someone that old? She was trying to find the daddy she never had.

I realize that many of these case studies repeat the theme of an unaffectionate father who causes a daughter to grow up and pursue destructive behavior. But I repeat it without apology because I see it all the time. If parents want to do something truly constructive to prevent their daughters from growing up to be super pleasers who fall into the hands of Punishing Controllers, misogynists, or Super Rats, they can do no better than to sit down and talk through how Daddy can give his daughter the support, affection, and love she needs, particularly in these tender, early adolescent years.

Barbara's second marriage hadn't worked, even though she had made a supreme sacrifice to keep a man who was eleven years older. While dating Ralph, she got pregnant and had an abortion at his insistence. Later they did get

243

married, but four years and no children later he deserted her without a trace.

By the time Barbara married Dean, she was a real pro at taking blame and feeling guilty. That's why he could dangle her on his string of criticisms and put-downs, or ignore her completely if he so chose. Dean was something of an emotional oaf, and like any Super Controller, he saw himself as the most important person in existence.

I worked hard with Barbara to help her learn how to stop buying into Dean's boorish behavior. She was definitely in the Swamp of Discouragement and living with a controller who had turned into an alligator. The best way to tame a controlling alligator is to separate his behavior from yours. When he acts like an oaf or is totally illogical or unreasonable, it is *his* problem.

For example, Barbara learned not to take the bait when Dean was silent and tuned out. Instead of begging him to talk or trying to use the "surefire conversation starters" that worked so well in real estate sales, Barbara was civil but never servile. If she needed conversation she would call a girlfriend, and when push came to shove, there was always television.

Equally important was helping Barbara combat Dean's alcohol-inspired barrages of criticism and complaints. I told her, "Don't sit or stand there lapping it up with the same old knee-jerk reaction. Step back mentally—and physically, if necessary—and stop to think. For example, suppose you're eating dinner and the carrots are overcooked. They really don't taste too good. What would Dean probably say?"

Barbara laughed. "As a matter of fact, that's exactly what happened a few nights ago. He told me the veggies tasted lousy, that I was a lousy cook, that I always had been, and I always would be."

"And what was your reaction?"

"Well, I got embarrassed and told him I was sorry, I'd try to do better next time. In fact, I even offered to cook a new batch of veggies."

"Very understandable. But with your new behavior mode you aren't going to buy that same old abuse anymore. Next time something like that comes up, try saying, 'You know, you're right. These veggies *are* lousy. I just left them on too long, I guess. How is your steak? Mine is perfect!'"

Barbara caught on quickly, and began using cognitive self-discipline to stop and think when Dean tried to play his controller games. She saw that Dean's controlling power over her was directly related to her willingness to always take the blame. Instead of absorbing blame like a sponge absorbs water, she started telling herself, *Wait a minute . . . I'm not to blame for his boring job or his lousy luck fishing. I don't have to listen to this.*

When Dean became belligerent and nasty and started to cut Barbara down, she learned to walk away, and even leave their apartment, if necessary. Barbara started going to a movie by herself or calling a girlfriend to go out shopping instead of listening to Dean's childish tirades or subjecting herself to stony silence. When she couldn't leave, and had to hear his criticisms, she started to respond with thoughts such as, *My goodness, he is mad at me and upset—but he doesn't really have a reason.*

I encouraged Barbara by pointing out, "Realize that the controlling man has a need to control and dominate you, and he'll attack you verbally or even physically to achieve his goals. But you can't be held accountable for his behavior. You can't buy into what he's doing because it is not your fault. When he starts that kind of thing, you have to walk away—and the quicker the better."

As Barbara continued to develop her new behavior and life-style, she hit highs and lows. On many occasions the "new Barbara" was overwhelmed by the "old Barbara," who still bought into Dean's abuse. Handling his silence was actually harder than handling his tirades and criticism. But she made progress, always hoping that by refusing to play Dean's games she would help him grow up and become a more mature husband. But once he learned that he could no longer control her, he simply couldn't handle it. Eventually, he left and she filed for divorce.

Less than a year later, Barbara stopped in to see me again because she was thinking of marrying another man she had been dating. It took me only two sessions to show her that she was headed for another "tow truck marriage." This man was even more emotionally oblivious than Dean had been. He didn't need mere fixing, he needed an emotional tow truck, and Barbara would have had to play the role.

From Barbara's description, it was apparent that she was putting forth far more than half of the effort to sustain the relationship. I suggested that she back off a bit and see if her new lover really wanted to carry the ball and his end of the relationship. She soon discovered that he had no intention of doing that at all. She broke off with him and was happier for it.

I hesitate to say it, but Barbara is a woman who probably should not marry again. She will function best in the business world as a single person and enjoy male and female companions as friends. But she is not a good risk for marriage because she is psychologically addicted to bringing home the losers of life.

If Barbara could stay out of relationships for about four years, she might develop the strength to have a fulfilling relationship with a noncontrolling man.

Why I Kicked Linda out of Therapy

Draining any kind of swamp always involves problems, delays, and even disasters. Swamps do not drain easily, especially swamps of discouragement where super pleasers have not been making any waves. When you start draining your swamp, you must be ready for the long haul. Controllers don't give up easily. They are willing to wait out pleasers, and that is why *you must expect opposition and be prepared to persevere and conquer it.*

Linda was a good case in point. She was thirty-four, mother of two small children, and separated from her husband when she came to see me on the advice of her parish priest. Her husband, Carlos, thirty-one, was a cocaine user who had been sleeping with other women for the past three years and now he was saying he wanted a divorce. However, what Carlos said and what Carlos did were poles apart. He would stay at his girlfriend's house (or sometimes his mother's), get high, and then wander home to raid Linda's refrigerator and then crawl in bed to have sex with her.

A super pleaser who would do anything to avoid conflict, Linda was barely making a living as a full-time clerk in a variety-goods store. Each time Carlos came back, she let him make all his usual promises about getting off drugs and coming home for good. Linda saw sex as an obligation and let Carlos use her when he chose. She was something of a Martha Luther and often played mother to Carlos, listening to his confessions and promises, assuring him he was okay, and giving him what he wanted: free food, free sex, and a free bed.

After staying a few days, Carlos would leave again and the whole ridiculous cycle would be repeated.

I told Linda she was acting as though she were the one who was a little crazy. "You ought to see a good psychologist," I quipped, after hearing about another Carlos escapade.

"You were the best I could find," she came back. "What can I do? I don't believe in divorce and I'm sick with guilt, just thinking about putting our kids through all that."

"What you have going right now is not exactly helping them," I pointed out. "You're being too easy on Carlos. He's like a lot of men who think sex solves everything. Every time you let him come home and have sex with you, he thinks you have forgiven him and that the problem is over. You must get him out of your life for a while—really put him to the test concerning all his promises to give up drugs."

"I don't know how to keep him away—I'm not even sure I can do it. . . ."

"Linda, you're in a no-win situation, with no hope for improvement unless you decide to take some action and make your needs and the needs of your kids important for once. You aren't facing reality, and Carlos will keep putting you through this sick nightmare indefinitely as long as you buy into his behavior."

"I'm not sure I follow you. How am I buying into what he does? He's the drug addict—"

"Yes, and you are the one who lets him come back, eat the food he hasn't provided, and make promises that are all lies. You know he's lying, but you keep buying into it—believing that somehow it might all be different. Carlos has you in his pocket. He dangles you like a little puppet on a string."

"But it's hard to say no to him," Linda said as she started to cry. "In spite of everything he's done I still love him and want to make love with him."

248

"I understand that, but the reality is that he is out tom-catting around with any number of women and there is no telling what he might bring home—venereal disease, herpes, even AIDS. You have to shut him off and stop being physically intimate with him."

Since Carlos had just left again, I told Linda now was the ideal time to change the locks on the house. That way she could start holding him accountable for his actions. Linda had the locks changed and a turning point came when Carlos wandered back home not too many nights later, put his key in the door, and found it didn't work. I had warned Linda that he might huff and puff and even start shouting and screaming, which he did. But she was ready with a restraining order and called the police, who made it clear to him he was to go away and not come back.

It was a major breakthrough. I advised Linda to keep Carlos away at least six months—he was not to see the children or her during that entire time.

"Above all else, stay out of bed with him!" I told her. "If he phones, hang up. Don't have any contact with him whatsoever."

What followed was as predictable as Tucson weather in August: heat and more heat. As soon as Linda withdrew from Carlos, he came on all the stronger. Presents started coming in the mail along with letters and cards. And, of course, he continued to try to phone.

Carlos wasn't giving up. The controller didn't want the pleaser to change, and he was doing his best to lure her back into the old sick swamp where he could play his games.

Linda started to weaken. She would come to the office and say, "Will you pray for me? You have to help me. I am weak today."

I told her the last thing she needed was to have her psychologist run interference for her. She had to stand on her own feet, make her own decisions, and stick to them.

"I made the six-month rule because you need at least that long to have any real effect on a man like Carlos. He's a drug user and he'll lie and cheat and do anything he can to get what he wants, which is more kicks."

But Linda couldn't hold out. She started to break the six-month rule. First, it was talking to Carlos on the phone . . . then he came over for "just a little while to see the kids." And, in no time at all he had her back in bed.

There are times when a psychologist has to take his own advice. Linda was getting opposition from Carlos, but I was getting opposition from Linda. She wasn't taking my advice and it was time for drastic action. I told her I wasn't going to see her anymore.

"You mean you're kicking me out of counseling?" said Linda, her mouth agape.

"That's exactly what I'm doing. I give you good, sound psychological counsel, and what do you do? You ignore it. I can't help you if you go on like this." I gave her the names of three other psychologists to choose from.

"Well, I can't help it," she defended herself. "I get lonesome."

"Do you want to get herpes?"

"Well, of course I don't, but I don't think that will happen. . . ."

"That's obvious. Do you really want your husband back? Do you want your children to have a father?"

"Well, sure, yes, of course I do."

"I wonder. I wonder if you really want this marriage to work. Maybe all you want to be is a victim and have people say, 'Oh, Linda, how do you put up with it all?'"

Linda left my office an extremely angry woman—possibly more angry than she'd ever been in her life. Two months went by and I didn't hear a word from her. I second-guessed myself several times and thought I might have made a serious error. But finally she phoned and said, "Now I see why you didn't want to see me any longer. You were right. It's worse than ever. Now I'm ready to give your plan a real try."

I agreed to see Linda, and this time she stuck with the plan. This time Carlos's opposition didn't break her down. She was firm. She put distance between herself and Carlos, and when he saw that he could get nowhere, he made the decision to do something about his drug problem. He checked into a treatment center and got his life straightened out. Today, Carlos has been clean for over a year. He and Linda are back together and their marriage continues to get better just a little bit at a time. Chaos has turned into cooperation, and they are going to make it.

What made the difference? Linda persevered. She didn't let the opposition and the problems break down her conviction and commitment.

When a pleaser decides to start saying no, and to refuse to continue playing her placating role, she can expect rough weather ahead. Husbands and children are not going to cheer her on. In fact, they are almost sure to get worse. They will give her more "controller shots" than ever because they want her to knuckle under and go back to being that "lovable pleaser" they can use and abuse.

When things get worse take heart; *you are on the right track.* Never give in to the ploys and pressures of people who are trying to get you to give up your attempts to change and make you go back to the same old familiar routine.

With Linda, I had to do what I call "pulling the rug out"— that is, take drastic action to show her I meant business.

And once I pulled the rug on Linda, she was able to pull the rug on Carlos, which forced him to make the changes that only he could make for himself. Carlos stopped being a controller who was interested only in his own desires and needs. He is working on becoming a caring husband.

And Linda is no longer the Depressed, Supersuffering Pleaser. She is climbing the Pyramid, and I think that someday she'll reach that upper Positive Pleaser level. At least she has drained the swamp, tamed the alligator, and knows what it's like to be pleased herself for a change.

As Susan Forward says, "There is no contradiction between being a loving, giving woman and taking care of yourself and acting in your own best interests. The most wonderful gift that you can give yourself and any man you become involved with is your sense of self-worth and, with it, your expectation of love and good treatment."[1]

You Probably Need One More Strategy

The strategies discussed in these last two chapters can be helpful to the woman caught in a painful or depressing marriage, but they are not a magic formula. A lot of marital swamps are baffling, difficult—even dangerous. If you're in a Controller Swamp that is getting too deep, I urge you to consider one more important strategy:

Get Some Help

The natural reaction that most people have when they suffer family problems is embarrassment and shame. They resolve to "deal with it myself." Sometimes this works. Sometimes a husband responds to his wife's new behavior and backs off. In fact, as we have seen in several case studies, the wife's stock goes up and the marriage improves. But note that all of my examples concern women *who came for therapy*. They had tried to handle it alone and had hit a dead end. They needed counsel, help, and support.

After twenty years of giving all three, I'm convinced that in many cases what people need most is support—encouragement from someone who is in their corner.

If you are in a situation where a Super Punishing Controller is making you miserable, afraid, and depressed, get some help, and fast. Your first step may be talking to a good friend. Perhaps your pastor can help. And beyond that are any number of professional resources.

If money is a problem, don't let it stop you. Counseling is available in every price range, from free to expensive. Whatever you do, *don't go it alone.*

PART 4

Portrait of a More Positive Pleaser

Our last two chapters invite you to consider a life-determining question: Do I *have* to please or do I *choose* to please?

Answer this question for yourself and you will have the secret to climbing out of the lower levels of the Pyramid of Pleasers and heading for the summit, where life is much more positive. You may not see yourself in a Swamp of Discouragement, but you are interested in escaping that steambath of exhaustion where many Played-Out Pleasers swelter. Or maybe you are at that Slightly Discouraged level and curious about how to get those pebbles of disrespect and being taken a little too much for granted out of your shoe. Then read on and discover

- the way to make "Choice Power" pay off
- how "bone digging" can bury a marriage
- why it's blessed to get as well as give
- how to let him know what you need
- how to help him express feelings, too
- why phony self-denial solves nothing
- how to "pull the rug out" by doing the unexpected
- a short course in learning how to say no
- how you can become assertive, not aggressive
- why every pleaser needs her priority slide rule
- how faith becomes your greatest resource

11

How to Use "Choice Power" to Become a Positive Pleaser

"Does the woman always have to give in?"

As I shared in chapter 2, a major premise of mine is that the "grain" of your personality was set in childhood, like the grain in a piece of wood. You cannot change your grain, but *you can change how you act and behave.* You are a pleaser, yes, but you are not doomed to going through life pleasing your husband and others because you *have* to. You can please because you *choose* to. In other words, you do not please out of fear, guilt, insecurity, and low self-esteem. You please out of high self-esteem, a good self-image, a strong faith, a healthy hope, and unconditional love.

The figurative Pyramid of Pleasers we've been using throughout this book is only a gauge to help you take some general bearings on where you feel you are right now. If you are at the Supersuffering or Depressed levels, talking about becoming a Positive Pleaser may sound like a lot of gobbledygook. You should go back to square one (chapters 9 and 10) and determine your next move, which might well be seeing a professional counselor.

Suppose, however, you see yourself somewhere in the middle of the Pyramid or closer to the top. You feel a bit played out, and at times exhausted, because you know you are running too fast and too hard to keep everybody happy. Perhaps you're just slightly discouraged and would appreciate a few ideas on how to be more assertive and confident. Or maybe you're enjoying the rarified atmosphere of Positive Pleaser, and you'd like a few more tips on how to stay up there.

That's what these last two chapters are about: using "Choice Power" to become and remain a more Positive Pleaser. We are, after all, the sum total of our choices. We can choose to act or choose to do nothing. The Positive Pleaser does not let others make her choices for her. She makes her own decisions about the kind of life she wants to live.

Choice Power for pleasers involves many areas, but we will focus on only four. This chapter will concentrate on choosing to take a risk, and choosing to give and get. Chapter 12 will cover choosing to please yourself, and choosing to set your own priorities.

Fear Often Hides "Under the Rug"

For any pleaser who wants to deal more confidently in a controller's world, risk has to be the name of the game. And fear is one of her most formidable foes.

I often tell clients, "You have to stop sweeping it under the rug." The "it" is whatever is making the pleaser feel put down, unloved, disrespected, or any number of other feelings that go with low self-image and lack of self-esteem.

The pleaser is prone to say, "It's okay . . . it doesn't matter . . . it's my fault . . . I'm to blame . . . he's not going to change anyway . . . I don't want to get him upset . . . there is no point in making anybody angry. . . ."

Fear keeps the pleaser trapped. To paraphrase some well-known advice, "The pleaser has nothing to fear but (her own) fear itself."

Pleasers often think, *Well, I tried to change—once—but all I got for my trouble was a put-down.* Or perhaps they got worse—embarrassed, chewed out, ignored, snubbed, or physically clobbered. Pleasers have tested the waters of life and found them full of sharks. It's better to stay on shore than venture out into the deep.

A striking illustration of what fear can do to a pleaser—and to her marriage—was the case of Melodie, who lived in fear with Ed for seventeen years because both of them preferred to avoid a problem rather than risk dealing with it and settling it once and for all.

Melodie came from a home where she got plenty of love and support from both parents. When Melodie married she wasn't unconsciously looking for a man who would abuse, neglect, or ignore her. What she failed to recognize in Ed was how certain amounts of alcohol could radically change his personality.

Early in their relationship and during the first seven years of their marriage, Ed drank little or not at all. But as he climbed toward middle-management positions at work, the pressure and tension mounted. Ed started having a glass of wine now and then. One Friday night after a stress-filled week at work, he had a second glass and was working on a third. Melodie started to chide him about it, not realizing he had moved past the "safe" level and was in the "red zone." Without warning, he smashed her on the side of her face with a closed fist and sent her reeling into a wall and then to the floor.

Melodie lay stunned for a few moments, then in terror she picked up her two-year-old son and fled the house.

It took Melodie several days to muster the courage to return home to Ed, who kept calling and wondering what was wrong and why she wouldn't come back. A few things that were "wrong" included a minor concussion, a broken nose, and some loose teeth. But damaged far more seriously were Melodie's pleaser emotions. She had grown up in a loving home where pleasing had always paid off. She liked the security of having things run smoothly and perfectly. When Ed's fist smashed into her face, something crumbled deep inside. She lived in fear from that moment on.

Unfortunately, when she did come home, neither of them dealt with the problem in any depth. They both swept it under the rug, with Ed making an embarrassed apology: "I don't know why I hit you—I guess I just had too much to drink. It won't happen again."

And it didn't—at least the hitting never happened again. Ed continued to do some drinking over the next few years but was careful to limit the amount. When he finally reached a plateau at work where he matched his ambitions with reality, he took a lot of pressure off himself and decided he didn't need to drink at all from that point on.

Through it all, however, Melodie lived in fear. During that time before Ed quit drinking completely, Melodie's heart would beat faster whenever she saw him pour a glass of wine with dinner. The very sight of Ed sipping alcohol made her tense and nervous. And when he showed brief flashes of temper because of pressures at work, or other frustrations, Melodie practically trembled.

Melodie Was an Expert Bone Digger

For seventeen years Melodie lived as though the clock had never ticked since that moment Ed struck her. And during those seventeen years she became an expert "bone digger." The bone digger is someone who, for whatever reason, will go back in the history of the marriage or the relationship and dig up a "bone of contention." It may have been a hassle, it may have been some kind of disappointment or betrayal. Whatever the problem, the bone digger continues to throw it in the mate's face. The bone is never dealt with and buried permanently. It always lies just below the surface and is dug up on demand.

Ed was really a very gentle man (as long as he stayed away from alcohol). He would probably have scored around 32 on the controller quiz in chapter 8, well below a true controller. He had a lot of flexibility, which made him a good bet for a husband.

In many ways, Melodie and Ed had a very good marriage, but it was marred by Melodie's bone digging—and, of course, her fear.

When Melodie finally came to see me, it was as much at Ed's request as it was her own idea. I worked with both of them over several months and eventually Melodie began to get a picture of what had really happened and why she had been so fearful ever since.

An only child, the apple of her parents' eye, Melodie was a quiet perfectionist. When the smooth waters of her marriage had turned into a momentary hurricane, she simply didn't know how to handle it. She fled the house that night but, more important, she fled emotionally in the years that followed.

As for Ed, he simply hadn't been able to understand what was really wrong. He thought he had apologized for striking Melodie and that that had been the end of it. He never liked it when Melodie kept digging up that bone labeled "When You Hit Me," but he always dismissed it as something she would do when tense or tired.

For seventeen years Melodie had been content to keep throwing the bone in Ed's face, but both of them had avoided the real problem, which was that Ed had hit Melodie and she had never forgiven him. This is a good example of how hard it is to recover from a major problem in a marriage. In counseling, they both finally realized that they had swept a huge bag of emotional garbage under the rug and had been tripping on it ever since.

It was a touching moment when Ed turned to Melodie and, with tears in his eyes, asked her total and complete forgiveness for what he had done. He finally realized how much he had hurt her and the agony she had been through.

For any counselor, it was a beautiful scene: two people who had been married almost twenty-five years, sitting in my office weeping and embracing. Melodie and Ed truly loved each other and had a marriage that was better than most. But that marriage could have been even happier had they dealt with their problem early on.

It is difficult to understand why we live with our fears and hang-ups as long as we do. For some reason, we prefer the familiar to the risk of changing our situation for the better. The guilt, fear, and pain are more comfortable than risking change. Perhaps we are lazy; maybe the fear of the unknown is too strong.

Whatever the reason, helping people change their behavior is a most difficult task. But when there is a breakthrough, I am reassured that I am in the right profession. Frequently I get notes from people who say in different ways, "Thank you for helping us turn it around." I keep those notes handy in a drawer of my desk and on days when I feel discouraged, I reach into that drawer and get a powerful lift from remembering the people, their problems, and the outcome of our sessions. I can often recall practically verbatim what those sessions were like. Their thank yous are therapy that keep *me* going.

You Can Learn How to "Risk It"

Granted, the story of Melodie and Ed is an extreme example of how we can let our fears prevent us from taking necessary risks. But the principle is still the same. Life has dealt us some kind of blow. What are we going to do about it?

Continuing the same pleaser routine is no answer. We must somehow muster the courage to take even a tiny risk of some kind if we want to change. If you want to read more about taking risks, I highly recommend *Risking* by David Viscott, M.D. Called "America's foremost commonsense psychiatrist," Dr. Viscott has written an easy-to-understand book that can help you face making crucial choices in life.

One of the best chapters in *Risking* includes a number of questions you can ask yourself as you prepare to take risks of all kinds, from buying a house to getting involved with someone. I've adapted a few of Dr. Viscott's questions, and added some of my own commentary. We could call the following exercise:

A Pleaser's Guide for Taking Risks

1. *Is this risk necessary?* (If you are a pleaser who is tired of being controlled, the answer is almost always yes.)

2. *Can I reach my goal in another way?* (Good question, but if there is another way to reach your goal, it will probably involve another risk!)

3. *What can I lose?* (Another good question. Think it through. What will this confrontation between the pleaser [you] and the controller [your husband, child, friend, boss] possibly cost? Your teeth? A large chunk of your peace and quiet? A friendship? Your job? Taking a risk does not mean you have to commit suicide. A pleaser, especially, should take bite-size risks and then reach out from there to take still bigger bites as confidence grows.)

4. *Who wants me to succeed at this risk?* (In many cases, you may be the only one. It is quite likely that the controllers who have you in their pockets will want you to fail. Or, it may be possible that a lot of those controllers don't even know they have you in their pockets. They are just going about their assertive, aggressive business and aren't really aware of how you feel. As mentioned in chapter 10, it always helps to get someone in your corner—a good friend, a pastor, or a professional counselor.)

5. *What feeling am I trying to express in taking this risk?* (Think this one through very carefully. You may want to review chapters 4, 5, and 6, which deal with low self-esteem, guilt, and perfectionism. By taking this particular risk, are you trying to make a statement about your self-image? Are you trying to shake the effects of false guilt and the guilt trip you've been on because a controller did a number on you? Perhaps you are trying to risk "not being perfect." What feeling are you after—freedom? accomplishment? relief?)

6. *If I take this risk, will people think better or worse of me—and do I care?* (It's quite likely some people will think better of you and others will think worse, particularly the controllers who don't want you to make any waves. Think on it hard: the fear of what people will think is powerful and numbing, especially for the pleaser. Remember, you are on a new track, seeking to change a behavior that you have engaged in for years. What other people think may have some importance, but it's not anywhere near as important as what *you* think.)

7. *Am I afraid?* (If the answer is yes, spell out what or who you are afraid of. Do you fear actual dangers or are your fears really products of your imagination and negative self-talk?)

8. *How much can I change because of this risk?* (Is the risk worth the step of change you seek in your life? If the step seems too large, how can you cut it down to manageable size? How badly do you want to change? Will the change be worth the stress and possible pain you will go through?)[1]

David Viscott points out:

> Only when you can admit that you want more than you have been getting, and only when the pain of your life is allowed to settle in on you like an unwelcome guest can you gather your forces and change. How long it takes depends on you.
> No one can make you change.
> No one can stop you from changing.
> No one really knows how you must change.
> Not even you.
> Not until you start.[2]

It Is Blessed to Give—and Get

Are you a giver or a taker? The pleaser sees the question as practically superfluous. Of course she is a giver. That's all she has been doing for years—while her husband, kids, friends, bosses, and everybody else takes and takes and takes some more.

In *Necessary Losses*, Judith Viorst observes that men generally want autonomy while women long for intimacy, and this crucial difference between the sexes helps explain why women often complain more about their marriages than men do.

Viorst goes on to say that various studies consistently show that wives express more marital discontent than do their husbands:

- More negative feelings and more marital problems
- More unhappiness and regret about the marriage
- More thoughts about separation or divorce
- More feelings of having to conform to expectations
- More frustration over making concessions and adaptations
- More depression, phobias, and emotional problems

She quotes sociologist Jessie Bernard, who has concluded that the cost of marriage is higher for wives than for husbands. If you are talking about good mental health and psychological well-being, the men have it better every time.

Despite all of their complaints about marriage, *more women than men find marriage a source of happiness*. They cling to marriage regardless of the cost.[3]

Down through the centuries women have been the pleasers, men the controllers. Robert Karen, who conducts workshops for men and women on power and intimacy, refers to the "old" and "new" systems of male/female relationships. Our parents and grandparents knew a world that had stabler values and much more clearly defined roles for men and women. Power and responsibility were assigned, and everyone knew where he or she stood. The system was often unfair to women but it did offer them a certain amount of security. If a woman was willing to accept the ground rules and the limits that marriage imposed on her, she could be quite happy.

A woman's job was to keep the home, raise the children, and be there for the whole family. The man's job was to go out and earn the living and "make contributions to society." Men were, in effect, put on a pedestal and wives were relegated to second-class citizenship.[4]

Enter women's liberation in the latter part of the twentieth century, and all this inequality is supposed to be dying out—but is it?

Women are finding that "having it all" is nothing that special. In fact, they are catching up with the men in having heart disease, ulcers, and other stress-related illnesses. Now they are allowed to get good jobs and earn excellent incomes, but the emotional balance of power at home is still much the same.

Most women still do the giving, while the men continue to take. The woman is the one who is more capable of compassion, support, and being there when needed. Men still aren't in touch with their feelings the way women are. They are less capable of reaching out to make emotional contact. But they are very capable of reaching out to take whatever a woman has to offer, and in so doing, they often take advantage.

Sandy Gave and Eric Took Until . . .

Sandy, a twenty-two-year-old graduate student, developed an intense relationship with Eric, twenty-five, who was in medical school. They didn't exactly live together, but Sandy's apartment was open to Eric at all times. She prided herself on making him dinners and washing and ironing the clothes he dropped off. She really loved to mother him.

Unfortunately, Eric was a Rat. He would call and arrange a date for dinner and then not show up for hours or not at all. Sandy's friends tried to warn her about Eric's reputation with women, but like a true pleaser, she loyally defended him. She preferred to believe only what she wanted to believe and preserve the romantic fantasy she thought she was living.

When Sandy came to me for counseling after a series of ups and downs, I found she was a first-born daughter with two younger brothers and a younger sister. Her relationship to her father and her mother had been good and her parents were happily married. She came from a family of achievers, and as the first-born daughter she was trying to live up to all kinds of expectancies and plans that her parents had for her, and that she had for herself as well.

But the giver was being used by the taker. Eric would come over to Sandy's apartment and the routine would always be the same. First she would feed him, then they would have sex, then they would watch TV or listen to music.

The problem with letting a man continue to be a taker is that he gets bored rather easily. Sandy was devastated when a girlfriend confided that she saw Eric with another woman at a local bar. That's when Sandy came to see me. What could I do to help her get Eric back?

Frankly, I wasn't keenly interested in helping her "get Eric back." I tried to help her see what an honest relationship between a man and a woman is really all about. This was not a loving relationship. Eric was the user and Sandy was the "usee."

You already know my advice to Sandy: "Instead of confronting him with his two- and three-timing behavior, try shutting him off sexually for a short time. That way, you can get a good reading on whether Eric really loves you, the person, or does he really love the sex, the babying, the mothering, being fed, and having his clothes washed."

Sandy tried the experiment and at first Eric reacted true to form. The more she put him off, the more he came on. But it didn't take long until Eric tired of the new game. He decided to take his marbles and move on to the next giver. He had a lot of other girls to choose from, so why did he need Sandy?

Sandy learned the hard way that "all give and no get" is no way for a woman to live with a man. When I encouraged her at our final counseling session, I said, "You're hurt and even a little embarrassed by how Eric used you and left you, but you're going to make it. Next time around, be interested in what the guy can give you instead of just giving him everything you have for free. One of the best pieces of advice any single woman can follow is to stay out of bed."

The story of Sandy and Eric is a typical example of how the male can take while the female gives. Eric was a super-controlling type who wasn't interested in learning how to give much of anything to a woman. While most men still play the role of taker, they are not all as lecherous or selfish as Eric. If you are gentle and patient, there may be a lot you can do to teach your man to become more caring, tender, and giving.

You don't have to knock him off that pedestal where our culture has placed him somewhat against his will; instead, you can join him on a more equal basis. There are things you can do to break your own habits of giving, pleasing, and clinging out of need and insecurity as you help him learn to share and become more emotionally intimate. Try some of the following strategies and see what happens:

Recognize what you need from your man right now. Maybe you need to hear him say he's sorry. Maybe you need a little tenderness and a kiss, but not necessarily sex. Do not ignore your needs and write them off as selfish. *Let him know what you need*, gently but persistently.

Think about all the things you give him. What is he getting that he takes for granted much of the time? Don't be afraid to let him know, but try not to be angry or intense when you talk about it. You are not seeking to punish him or pick a fight; you are trying to help him see that the scales need to balance.

Be content with small steps of progress. Some men have trouble expressing emotions and showing feelings. I'm not suggesting that you be "thankful for small favors," which we discussed in chapter 4. Besides, you're not asking for a small favor; you're asking him to be vulnerable, perhaps for the first time in his life. Even if his first efforts in giving of himself aren't much, encourage him anyway.

Strike a balance between being honest with your man and still showing him respect. According to Willard Harley, one of the five basic needs of a man is to be respected by his wife and to feel that she is proud of him.[5] Let him know it's okay to express needs and even weaknesses. A lot of men are tired of playing the supermacho role and would welcome the chance to lean on someone else for a change, even just a little bit.

Monitor how much you're giving and try to cut back on always being so sweet and helpful. Look for ways to give him opportunities to give of himself. If you make agreements about the division of labor in the home, be sure he lives up to his side of the bargain.

For example, if you both work, you may decide that you'll do the basic cooking while he makes the coffee every morning. You may agree to clean the bathroom, but his job is to vacuum the apartment. In many cases these deals last all of two weeks. Then you're back to your old pleasing ways, doing everything. Don't let that happen. Don't vacuum, don't make coffee—and remind him of the original bargain.

Have faith in the principle that a person can change his or her behavior, and be willing to stand your ground. Here is where we come back to taking a risk. You want to preserve your relationship, yes, but you're also interested in *improving it.* After all, there is no reason *he* can't use Choice Power to become a more positive and caring controller.[6]

I deal with many pleasers who hesitate to even think about getting as well as giving. They are convinced that talking about "getting" smacks of self-indulgence, greed, and narcissism.

This kind of phony self-denial is one of the pleaser's major enemies. Susan Forward believes that the contemporary woman's goal should be holding on to the qualities that make her unique: intuition, being comfortable with feelings and emotions, and being a nurturer. She should let go of "those self-denying behaviors that have not served (her) well." To be a woman, says Forward, "no longer means to be passive, submissive and self-denigrating."[7]

I couldn't agree more. In our final chapter we'll look at more ways to use Choice Power to move away from false self-denial and toward becoming a Positive Pleaser.

12

How to Please Yourself without Feeling Guilty

"I think I do it because it's fun!"

Alma is a thirty-year-old single parent with two small children. She supplements child-support payments by caring for the children of women who are pursuing high-powered careers as legal secretaries, office managers, and executives. Alma gets paid very little and often must work well past the agreed-upon time for the mothers to return home.

The typical scenario sees one of these working mothers calling and telling Alma she has to work late and could Alma possibly stay with the kids until she gets there? Alma always agrees, because she's such a good sport, and around

1:00 a.m., or even later, the mother rolls in from "working late," often more than a little unsteady from an after-work nightcap.

When Alma came to see me, I advised her to tell these mothers she needed more pay and a better understanding of hours—overtime, for example, for anything past six o'clock, when the mothers were supposed to be home. But every time Alma plans to speak up, one of the mothers says something like, "Oh, the kids love you so much. You do such a tremendous job, we just don't know what we'd do without you. . . ."

"How can I confront them when they say such nice things?" wails Alma. "I know I'm being walked on but I don't know what I can do about it."

Alma is a pleaser who lives a discouraged life because she lacks what I call the "assertiveness edge." She doesn't know how to say no to unfair and inconsiderate demands; she prefers to simmer in her own juice rather than confront the controllers who are taking advantage of her.

In her excellent book *How to Be an Assertive (Not Aggressive) Woman in Life, in Love, and on the Job*, Jean Baer lists several kinds of woman who have problems being assertive with family, friends, or co-workers. Included in her lists are the *shrinking violet*, the *fear victim*, the *woman who wants the world to love her*, and the *split assertive*.[1] It's not hard to spot the pleaser in all of these.

The *shrinking violet* invites people to walk all over her because she can't stand up for herself. She seldom receives a thank-you for what she does, seldom expresses her opinions, and of course she never says no.

Ann, thirty-nine and the single parent of two teenagers, is a shrinking violet at her job as a nurse's aide in a hospital. Her floor supervisor has spotted her as a pleaser and constantly takes advantage of her. Ann always winds up with at least fifteen or more beds to take care of on a shift, while all of the other nurse's aides have fewer than ten. Ann's supervisor gives her plenty of verbal strokes by telling her she is a good worker, she can "work circles around the rest of the girls," and so on. But Ann only ends up with more to do and the same amount of pay.

Because she is so fed up, she comes home full of anger and frustration and then takes it out on her teenagers, which makes her feel worse than ever. She feels guilty enough because her children have no father (he deserted the family when they were very small). By the time Ann came to see me she was in a vicious downward cycle that revolved around anger, guilt, and depression. And every day at work it was the same old story. . . .

The *fear victim* goes about saying, "I'd like to, but I can't. I know I should, but I'm afraid." For the fear victim, just getting up in the morning is a major risk.

The *woman who wants the world to love her* is lacking in self-esteem. She wants everyone to think she's simply wonderful—her husband, her children, the boss, even all the salesmen who come to the door (and so she buys a lot of stuff she doesn't even want). She trades self-respect for praise and the reputation of being "such a nice person." Ann fits this profile quite well.

We've seen at least two cases of the *split assertive* in earlier chapters. She's the one who's a tiger at work and a mouse at home. A close cousin to the *split assertive* is the *brainwashed female*, who may be able to stand up to women but never to men. She is the topic of books such as *The Good Girl Syndrome*. She has been programmed to believe that men are top dogs and women are there to honor and obey them.

Become Your "Primary Project" for the Year

How about you? Yes, you are a pleaser, but you don't want to be shrinking, fearful, fawning, and needing approval. What can you do? Here are some practical tips:

1. *You must come to terms with any guilt you have about pleasing yourself.* I am not suggesting that you follow Robert Ringer down his self-centered path to looking out for Number One. Your primary goal in trying to please yourself is to even things up a bit. You are not after revenge and you have not sold your soul to the devil. You simply want to be a more positive person in every way. Remaining a pleaser who is Supersuffering, Depressed, Exhausted, or Discouraged is *not* being positive; it is being far less than a balanced—and joyful—person.

2. *Make yourself the "primary project" for the year.* That is, spend some time and money on yourself. Buy some new clothes or something else you've been wanting for a long time, like a new wall hanging for the study. Then wear those clothes and use whatever you buy. I counsel any number of women who buy a new dress, take it home, hang it in the closet, and after three or four days take it back to the store saying, "It just wasn't right for me. I want to return it." This isn't frugality; it is lack of self-worth. This kind of pleaser simply doesn't believe she deserves a new dress.

3. *Continuing the primary-project-for-the-year* idea, work out a schedule that gives you regular opportunities to be good to yourself: join a health spa and go once or twice a week; set aside Thursday afternoons to go to the library and just read and browse; arrange for Saturday mornings off to go shopping or whatever, while hubby brandishes whip and chair and bravely watches the children.

The possibilities are practically limitless. It all depends on what you feel would be good for you. If you still can't think of anything, just start brainstorming by using sentences that begin with phrases such as, "I've always wanted to . . ." or, "If I ever had the time I would. . . ." But instead of just dreaming, finish the sentence and then *do it*!

How Mary Lou Got Her Teenagers' Attention

Another good strategy for the pleaser is to do the unexpected. I often suggest "pulling the rug" from under people who are taking advantage of you in subtle or not-so-subtle ways. I'm not suggesting actual violence or trying to harm anyone. There are, however, a lot of ways to let the "takers for granted" know you want—and deserve—some TLC yourself for a change.

I recall Mary Lou, a single mom of thirty-eight who had teenagers sixteen and fourteen. Mary Lou worked full-time, so she tried to arrange for a division of labor at home. She assigned Brad and Pam to start preparing dinner by doing things such as setting the table, taking the chicken out of the freezer so it could thaw, putting on the potatoes to cook, and other easy jobs.

Brad and Pam nodded absently when given their instructions, but the next night when Mary Lou came home the table was unset, the chicken was unthawed, and the kids were on the phone, watching TV, and lost in that mysterious world of portable stereo and headphones.

Well, it wasn't quite true that they hadn't "prepared any food." Twinkie wrappers were everywhere, and somebody had shown real initiative in microwaving a frozen individual pizza. Mary Lou shouted constructive criticism: "I can never

277

count on you! Don't you care about your mother? When are you ever going to take some responsibility?"

All this tirade managed to get Mary Lou was a good case of the guilties for losing her temper, and no cooperation from Brad and Pam. The vicious cycle kept repeating itself, and finally Mary Lou came to see me.

"What we have here is a failure in discipline," I said. "You need to use some cognitive self-discipline on yourself and some Reality Discipline on your kids. The next time you come home and dinner is not in progress, just turn around and leave."

"Leave? Where am I going to go?"

"Why, out to dinner, of course."

"I can't go out to dinner. I've got to feed my kids. . . ."

"Listen to what you're saying. 'I've got to feed my kids.' You're locked in on that idea. It's set in concrete in your mind. I say you *don't* have to feed your kids. They are sixteen and fourteen years old and they will survive. Right now I'm more worried about *your* survival—go out to dinner!"

Mary Lou didn't have to wait long to try my advice. The very next evening she arrived home from an especially exhausting day at work to find the kitchen a shambles, Pam on the phone, and Brad out in the garage tinkering with his motorcycle.

"Hey, Ma, when's dinner?" somebody asked.

"For me, it's right now. I'm going out to eat. You can do what you like."

And with that, Mary Lou drove a few blocks to Coco's, where they make an excellent hamburger, and had a leisurely meal while she read the paper.

The next night she came home from work, and guess what? Was the table set? Were the potatoes baking merrily in the oven? Of course not. Nothing had changed—yet. So,

Mary Lou went out to dinner again. In fact, she had to do her disappearing act at least four times before it registered with her kids.

Finally, the Twinkie wrappers and pizza cartons and general mess got so deep that Brad and Pam started complaining. Didn't Mom love them anymore? What kind of a mother would treat her kids this way?

Mary Lou sat down with Pam and Brad and they had a little family council that led to a new pact. As long as the kids made a genuine effort to carry their part of the load, Mary Lou would not "desert" them in their dinner hour of greatest need. The whole family agreed to pull together and help one another.

A few weeks later Mary Lou reported back that the plan was really beginning to help. "There are nights when they still goof off," she said, "but all kids do that occasionally. Most of the time, though, they do their part, and on some nights they prepare the entire meal! We're getting somewhere at last."

A Short Course in Saying No

Every pleaser must become increasingly skilled at using the word *no*. Jean Baer's work on assertiveness has revealed that saying no is a learnable skill, and she points to research at the University of Wisconsin, which suggests the following principles.

1. It's best to start your answer to the request with the word *no*. If you hem and haw, you can be more easily wheedled into saying maybe or yes.
2. Be firm. Look the other person right in the eye and speak up. Don't verbally say no while you nonver-

bally say, "Well, I'll probably do it if you pressure me enough."

3. Be brief. Don't go on and on with apologies or reasons you can't comply with. It will only put you on the defensive, and you may start to weaken and eventually give in.[2]

Life is full of opportunities to practice saying no. For example, a telephone salesman calls and starts to give you an unwanted pitch about investments or insurance. If you say, "Well, I think we already have enough insurance," you only give him a chance to go to square two. But if you say, "No, I am not interested," he will hang up.

A good friend of mine once confessed to me that his favorite way to handle telephone sales calls is to throw the phone down on the floor and let the caller talk to the rug for a while. I wouldn't necessarily advise that kind of treatment of the phone or the caller, but I do admit there are times when it is tempting.

Or suppose your eight-year-old comes home and says, "Mom, can I stay overnight at Jane's tonight?"

Instead of going into details about who Jane is, where she lives, and why your daughter wants to stay with her, simply point out, "No, it's a school night and you don't sleep over on school nights."

Then there is that time of the year when you hear the inevitable knock at your door and there stands that irresistible package known as the ten-year-old neighborhood cherub who is selling Girl Scout cookies. Instead of letting her go on and on with her charming spiel, brace yourself and gently say, "Sorry, honey, we're not buying any cookies this year. We still have fourteen boxes left from last year."

To be truthful, I'm a patsy for most little kids who come by hawking candy or other wares, usually wanting three or four dollars for something worth less than half of that. Sometimes I try to get off the hook by simply giving them a dollar bill, but even that doesn't always work. I once got into quite an argument with a nine-year-old entrepreneur who refused to take the dollar and kept saying, "The candy's four dollars."

"I know, I know," I finally said. "Just take the dollar and good luck in your career!"

The Difference between Assertive and Aggressive

Whenever you try pleasing yourself for a change, always work on being assertive but not aggressive. To be *assertive* means to make your own choices, stand up for your rights, but allow other people to have their rights, too. To be *aggressive* is to go on the offensive and usually become offensive as well. You don't necessarily honor the rights of others, and you may have a hidden agenda to want to humiliate, intimidate, or simply put somebody down.

For example, suppose you're standing in the supermarket line with a brimming cart of groceries. It's 5:30 p.m. and you're due home in fifteen minutes to get a complicated dinner started. The "twelve items or less" counter is closed, and now a second person comes up with a carton of milk and a loaf of bread and asks you if he can go on ahead.

An angry, aggressive answer would be something like this: "Absolutely not! I've got a schedule, too, and you'll have to wait your turn like everybody else!" (And then you stand there for the next five minutes and feel the person's eyes bore into the back of your head while you wait for your total to be rung up.)

A more assertive approach, however, would be something like this: "I'd like to let you in, but I have an extremely tight schedule and I've got to get checked out and get home. I'm afraid I can't help you. Why don't you try the next counter? Maybe that lady can help you."

The key to being assertive rather than aggressive is not necessarily in *what* is said but *how* it is said. If you are angry or uptight, it will come through as aggressive no matter what words you use. The assertive person keeps her cool and communicates clearly and honestly.

If you're used to being a pleaser, being aggressive may seem easier than being assertive. Sometimes it's easier to be angry, and "not let them push me around anymore!" But that approach will only lead you into gathering more guilt. Take small steps toward being assertive, and make it part of your new Positive Pleaser behavior.[3]

The Positive Pleaser Sets Her Own Priorities

If you have read any of my other books, you may be thinking, *Oh, oh, here he comes with his lecture on priorities.* You're right, but I prefer to call it commonsense advice, not a lecture. The cure to "pleaseritis" is the same one I suggested in *Bonkers* for battling and preventing mother stress:

1. priorities
2. Priorities
3. PRIORITIES

There is a lot of good advice available on setting priorities. I especially like the ideas in *Strategy for Living* by Edward R. Dayton and Ted W. Engstrom, who point out that prioritizing is really a matter of setting the *right* goals and not setting *more* goals than you can handle.[4] Some good questions for any pleaser to ask herself are these:

How urgent is it? People often complain about living under "the tyranny of the urgent." Pleasers, of course, live under the tyranny of controllers who insist that their goals and priorities are the ones that are urgent.

An indispensable piece of equipment for every pleaser is what I call the "priority slide rule." When things come up, requests are made, or emergencies occur, the pleaser can whip out her slide rule and decide what must be done first, rather than dash madly about trying to do everything at once and "keep everyone happy."

A second crucial question is this: *How important is it?* Dwight Eisenhower has been quoted as saying, "The urgent is seldom important, and the important is seldom urgent." Some people like to live under the tyranny of the urgent. They enjoy "putting out fires." They breathlessly rush from one big problem to another—*everything* is important, and only they can handle it.

Pleasers often fall into this trap. Check yourself on how much "fire fighting" you've done lately. True, there are emergencies that must be taken care of now. There are urgent matters that cannot be delayed. But is *everything* in this category? To repeat the question, how important is it? Is it very important, quite important, somewhat important, or not very important at all?

As you rate all you must do in order of importance, you automatically start to prioritize. And you automatically force yourself back to why this certain "it" is there anyway. Maybe "it" doesn't really need doing at all.

And that brings us to our next question: *What will happen if it is not done at all?* Will there be trouble? Will a controller be upset? Will somebody think less of you? Will you have to take the blame or say it's all your fault?[5]

All of the above questions are excellent ways to practice cognitive self-discipline—standing back and thinking things through. Then you can avoid getting trapped by dwelling too much on the "big picture." In other words, don't schedule too much. In fact, start deliberately planning and scheduling what seems to be a lot less than you normally do. As already mentioned, start using the word *no*. It's amazing how well it works.

If you simply can't say no face-to-face to family or friends, practice by talking to yourself in the mirror, or try addressing an empty chair. Pretend your friend Alice is sitting there and say, "Alice, I'm sorry, I simply don't have time for that."

I know it sounds kooky, but it works. *Just saying the words out loud* is a start toward controlling your own life and becoming a positive, assertive pleaser rather than a perfectionistic, driven, and dominated pleaser who always feels as if the stampede has just come through her kitchen—again.

Another way to say no is to respond to a request with, "Let me think about it . . . pray about it . . . talk to John about it . . . and I'll get back to you." This way you have time to weigh what the request really means, how much time it will take, what John thinks about the idea, and to pray about it. I often tell clients who believe in prayer that if people did more praying about what they're deciding to get into, they wouldn't have to do so much pleading with God to get them out of it.

Don't Neglect the Greatest Resource of All

Speaking of God, I urge you to consider making Him the top priority in your life. You can read all kinds of self-help books, attend seminars, faithfully watch Oprah or Phil—in short, gather all the human wisdom available. But if you lack a spiritual connection to your Creator, you will continue to struggle with uncertainty and doubt.

On occasion I refer a client to a large globe of the world standing in my office. I suggest that she find North America, then the United States, Arizona, and finally, the tiny dot that represents Tucson. And then I say, "See that tiny dot? That represents almost a half million people, and you and I are two of them. I find it very reassuring that God unconditionally loves both of us as much as all the rest. We may think we have imperfections and that we are rather insignificant, but the truth is that each of us can have a relationship with the One who has made it all."

I meet many pleasers who are trapped in swamps of suffering, discouragement, and exhaustion because they have little or no faith. They wallow in low self-esteem, guilt, and timidity because they lack the spiritual resources to take action.

Do you want to be able to take a risk? Do you want to be able to get as well as give, especially in your relationship with your husband? Do you want to be able to please yourself without feeling guilty and without neglecting others? Do you want to be able to set your own priorities and organize your life to fit your needs and what you believe to be your purpose for living? Then do not fail to develop the spiritual side of who you are.

Today it is much in vogue to work on the physical as well as the emotional and the mental. But without the spiritual, you are out of balance. I'm not talking about an occasional visit to church or taking a long walk now and then to commune with nature. I'm talking about developing your understanding of and love for the One who made you, who knows you inside and out, who is familiar with all your ways. Before you think any thought, He already knows it. No matter where you go, He is there.[6]

Holly Taught Us about Faith Firsthand

C. S. Lewis said we must train our habit of faith. My wife, Sande, and I got a firsthand demonstration from our daughter Holly when she was only three. The Ringling Brothers Circus was coming to Tucson, and for weeks before it arrived, Holly watched TV ads inviting all the kids to ride the special circus train that would go around the inside of the arena. Holly watched all those TV clips showing little happy-faced children riding this special train, and announced, "I'm going to ride the train, too!"

Sande and I laughed and said, "Isn't that cute. She will forget all about it by circus day."

Holly didn't forget. The train was all she could think about. We tried to tactfully suggest that with nine thousand people there, most of whom would be kids, it might be hard to be chosen—"especially when you're only three and not that big."

But Holly's faith did not waver. Yes, she knew there would be lots of people, but she had her heart set on riding that train anyway.

As luck would have it, we got to the arena barely ahead of circus time. As we found our seats we learned that ushers had come through the crowd an hour before and picked all the children who would ride the special little train around the arena and officially open the circus performance. Holly could see the kids getting on the train far below near the center ring, and she started wondering when she was going to get on. We asked her if she would like some popcorn as we tried to explain that the train was already full.

But Holly's little face never stopped gleaming with excitement. Any moment she would get her ride on the train!

Her parents' faces were the picture of something a bit different. Any moment Holly would suffer the disappointment of her young life, and our family day at the circus would be ruined.

Just as the lights were being dimmed and the miniature steam engine was giving a few last warm-up toots, an usherette came up the aisle carrying a little girl about Holly's age, who was crying and wanting her mama. Handing the frightened tyke back to her mother, who was sitting in the row in front of us, the usherette looked up and spotted Holly. She looked right into Holly's eyes and asked, "Would you like to go on the train? There's one more seat."

Holly never said a word but shook her head yes and put her arms out to the usherette to be carried down the stairs. Just as they started down, Holly looked back over her shoulder at us as if to say, "O ye of little faith."

And so we watched Holly get carried to the train and placed in a seat. We watched as she rode around the arena, waving and laughing and having the ride of her life. Several times she looked up and waved to us, and then it hit me: For weeks she had been saying, "I'm going to ride on the train." When she had seen the TV spots advertising the circus, she had always said, "There's that train I'm going to ride on—just see if I don't."

When the usherette brought Holly back to us, all she said was, "That was fun, Daddy. Where's the popcorn?"

And so we had popcorn and more popcorn . . . and ice cream . . . and a magic gun . . . and hot dogs . . . and thirty-five dollars and three hours later we filed out into the late-afternoon sunshine. I felt just a little like one of the five thousand who had shared a certain little boy's lunch by the seashore. And I couldn't help but recall what Jesus once said about having the faith of a little child.

Portrait of a Positive Pleaser

I hope the story of a three-year-old's simple faith doesn't sound as if I'm trying to depreciate or oversimplify your problems. It's just that I am convinced that childlike faith is the secret to becoming a Positive Pleaser. Faith *is* Choice Power. By having faith to make your own choices, you can start to take those tiny risks. You can start saying no to the controllers, lovingly but positively.

The Positive Pleaser puts her faith into action every day. I've watched one do it for more than twenty years. My wife, Sande, who is called "Bucky" in our inner-family circle, has modeled positive pleasing throughout our marriage. She does not give because she has to but only because she wants to out of an overflow of love and joy and being satisfied with who she is.

And she certainly knows how to say no. Early in our marriage she said no to my sloppy ways and refused to let me pile my clothes wherever they happened to fall from my body. She said no to my picky eating habits and my tendency to sulk when I didn't get my way. And she said no to my clumsy pawing for sex and introduced me to what women call affection. (Even a young psychologist needs some training now and then.)

But over the years I've learned even more as I have watched Bucky say yes to doing things that touch other lives with love and concern.

Bucky is your consummate "doer of nice things for others"—from taking meals to sick friends to putting up singing groups who perform at our church and who need dinner and a place to stay. Recently, she really didn't have time to drive my mother forty-two miles through Tucson's traffic. (When you hear about sprawling cow towns, we're it—even the coyotes have rest stops.) But Mom needed new glasses and her car was in the shop. Bucky didn't have to take her—she could have called a cab—but she chose to do it because she cares.

She works all this into her "usual" schedule, which would have any bus driver asking for overtime. A typical run finds her getting Holly to guitar lessons, picking up Krissy at school, and dropping Kevey off for Little League practice, all with split-second timing within twenty-eight minutes during evening rush hour. (No, her minivan isn't yellow, it's brown and tan.)

How does Bucky avoid burnout? She has a husband who brings coffee to her bedside every morning. And I do pitch in. For being a baby brat, I even surprise myself sometimes! In addition, Bucky makes it a point to take a nap almost every weekday.

It's fun to live with the "Pizza Lady." Bucky got that title by answering the phone one evening and hearing about the need for people to help with serving pizza on Thursdays at noon to all the students in our children's school. Previous calls for volunteers had met with deafening silence. Could Bucky help them out? There wouldn't be a whole lot to it—just be there to meet the trucks when they delivered the four hundred slices of pizza, and then distribute it to all those hungry little urchins who turn into piranhas at the sight of pepperoni floating in hot mozzarella.

Bucky's first reaction to helping solve the pizza crisis was reluctance. She already had plenty of things going and Thursdays were especially busy. As she hung up the phone she told the caller, "Well, try to get someone else, but if you can't, I'll be happy to do it."

I chuckled silently behind my sports page. How naïve could a pleaser get? Did Bucky think that with such an open-ended response, they would call forty other people? She would get a call in the morning to let her know, "We couldn't get anybody else."

Sure enough, the call came through and, naturally, so did Bucky. She took the job, which she has held for the past school year. Every Thursday morning she gets to the school just before eleven thirty to meet the first shipment of pizza, which is delivered by the "Pizza Factory," one of Tucson's premier pizza producers.

She lines up the twelve pans of pizza in the little lunch trailer on the school grounds and awaits the first wave of hungry kids who have paid the teacher the money and gotten their special ticket, redeemable with the "Pizza Lady" for one slice of hot, delicious pizza.

Because it is located in the deserts of southern Arizona, the last time Tucson had a really cool day was during the Ice Age. Naturally, around the noon hour it gets quite warm in the little lunch trailer, which is air-cooled by a tiny six-inch fan. Bucky smiles through it all as she dispenses pizza and cold drinks. She counsels tearful children who have strange tales to tell: "A cat tinkled on my pizza ticket!" "My dog ate my ticket." And she often serves pizza to little boys with a big smile while whispering discreetly under her breath, "Your zipper is open."

After the first twelve pans are gone and the first wave of pizza snackers have returned to class, Bucky gathers up the empty pans, meets the second delivery truck from the Pizza Factory, and sets up for round two with twelve more pans of pizza. When all of it is gone, she packs up the pans, puts them in her car, and returns them to the Pizza Factory on the way home.

"Bucky," I asked after she described a particularly wild pizza day at school, "why do you do this? What's in it for you, besides a free slice of pizza if there is any left over?"

Bucky thought for a few moments before answering. "You know, that's a good question. I don't have to do this. I'm already homeroom mother and do lots of special favors for the school all the time. Basically, I think I do it because I enjoy being with the kids—especially the junior high boys, who like to think they give me a hard time. I have a real friendship going with some of them."

Thinking I might as well do a little research on my *Pleasers* manuscript, I pressed her and said, "C'mon, you know you're a pleaser—don't you do it to please the school and the mothers and the kids?"

"No, I really don't. I think I do it to please myself. Besides, I think I'm lucky to be at home and not working and to have time for things that many other mothers would like to do but can't. I feel as if I'm meeting a real need down there, and I think it sets a good example for our kids."

"But you don't seem to get many thank-yous."

"I'd really be embarrassed to get a lot of thank-yous or be recognized on Awards Day at the end of the year." And then she added with a wink, "I really don't need a reward. I do what I do because it's fun, and I know I'm filling a need at the school. Besides, the Pizza Factory makes great pizza!"

Maybe that's the bottom line for every pleaser. Whatever you do to please, be sure it's fun for you as well as everyone else. And enjoy the view from the top of the Pyramid!

Game Plan for Pleasers

Finish every day and be done with it. You have done what you could. Some blunders and absurdities no doubt crept in; forget them as soon as you can. Tomorrow is a new day; begin it well and serenely and with too high a spirit to be cumbered with your old nonsense. This day is all that is good and fair. It is too dear, with its hopes and invitations, to waste a moment on yesterdays.

Ralph Waldo Emerson

Notes

Chapter 1 What Kind of Pleaser Are You?

1. William Fezler and Eleanor S. Field, *The Good Girl Syndrome* (New York: Macmillan Publishing Company, 1986), p. xi.

2. Ibid., p. xiii.

3. Robin Norwood, *Women Who Love Too Much* (New York: Pocket Books, a Division of Simon & Schuster, Inc., 1986). Doctor Susan Forward and Joan Torres, *Men Who Hate Women and the Women Who Love Them* (New York: Bantam Books, 1986).

Chapter 2 The Little Girl Who Lives in You

1. Suzanne Fields, *Like Father, Like Daughter* (Boston: Little, Brown and Company, 1983), see p. 6.

2. James J. Rue and Louise Shanahan, *Daddy's Girl, Mama's Boy* (Indianapolis: The Bobbs-Merrill Company, Inc., 1978), p. 63.

3. William S. Appleton, *Fathers and Daughters* (New York: Doubleday and Company, Inc., 1981), pp. 12–13.

4. See 2 Corinthians 5:17 NIV.

5. First Corinthians 13:11 NIV.

Chapter 3 Why a Pleaser Can Be Born Anytime

1. Alfred Adler, *Understanding Human Nature* (London: George Allen & Unwin Ltd., 1928), p. 149.

2. Ibid., p. 149.

3. See Bradford Wilson and George Edington, *First Child, Second Child* (New York: McGraw-Hill Book Company, 1981), p. 104.

4. Adler, *Understanding Human Nature*, p. 150.

5. Ibid., p. 156.

Chapter 4 Pleasers Battle a Low Self-Image

1. Alfred Adler, *The Practice and Theory of Individual Psychology* (London: Routledge & Kegan Paul, Ltd., 1923), p. 3.

2. Ibid., p. 3.

3. Herbert Fensterheim and Jean Baer, *Don't Say Yes When You Want to Say No* (New York: Dell Publishing Company, Inc., 1975).

4. Jean Baer, *How to Be an Assertive (Not Aggressive) Woman in Life, in Love, and on the Job* (New York: New American Library, a Signet Book, 1976).

5. See my book *Making Children Mind without Losing Yours* (Old Tappan, New Jersey: Fleming H. Revell Company, 1984).

6. Philippians 4:8 TLB.

7. Sonya Friedman, *Smart Cookies Don't Crumble* (New York: Pocket Books, 1986), see chapter 3.

Chapter 5 The Guilt Gatherers of Life

1. Susan Forward and Joan Torres, *Men Who Hate Women and the Women Who Love Them* (New York: Bantam Books, 1986), pp. 50–51.

2. David D. Burns, *Feeling Good* (New York: New American Library, a Signet Book, 1981), see pp. 178–79.

3. Ibid., pp. 32–33.

4. This is a quote by Gordon Allport in *Loving Free*, by Paula and Dick McDonald (New York: Ballantine Books, 1977), p. 118.

Chapter 6 Pleasers, Perfectionism, and the Avis Complex

1. Burns, *Feeling Good*, pp. 309–10.

2. Cherry Boone O'Neill, *Starving for Attention* (New York: Dell Publishing Company, Inc., 1983), p. 53.

3. James Calano and Jeff Salzman, *Real World 101* (New York: Warner Books, Inc., 1984), pp. 114–15.

4. Hans Selye, *The Stress of Life*, Revised Edition (New York: McGraw-Hill Book Company, 1978), p. 81.

5. Burns, *Feeling Good*, p. 310.

6. Ibid., pp. 325–26.

7. Kevin Leman, *The Birth Order Book* (Old Tappan, New Jersey: Fleming H. Revell Company, 1985), p. 70.

Chapter 7 Pleasers Are the Moths, Controllers Are the Flame

1. Willard Harley, *His Needs, Her Needs* (Old Tappan, New Jersey: Fleming H. Revell, 1986), p. 30.

2. Ibid., p. 29.

3. See "Women Getting AIDS through Sex Double in Five Years, Study Finds," *Los Angeles Times*, Friday, April 17, 1987, p. 20.

4. First Corinthians 13:4–7 TLB.

Chapter 8 Seeing Controllers "Up Close and Personal"

1. Sonya Friedman, *Men Are Just Desserts* (New York: Warner Books, Inc., 1983), pp. 7–10.

2. Ibid., p. xiii.

3. "Dear Abby: It's Smart to Keep Saying No to Sex," Abigail Van Buren, *The Arizona Daily Star*, Tuesday, April 7, 1987.

4. Elizabeth Mehren, "Unmarried: Making Sense of Singledom," *The Chicago Sun Times*, Sunday, March 8, 1987, p. 8.

5. Robin Norwood, *Women Who Love Too Much* (New York: Pocket Books, a Division of Simon & Schuster, Inc., 1986).

Chapter 9 Which Way Out of Controller Swamp?

1. See Forward and Torres, *Men Who Hate Women*, especially "Personal Introduction," pp. 11–12.

2. See Norwood, *Women Who Love Too Much*, especially chapter 1, "Loving the Man Who Doesn't Love Back," pp. 1–25.

3. Genesis 2:24 NIV.

4. Friedman, *Men Are Just Desserts*, p. 3.

5. Ann Landers, "Asking Hard Questions after the Affair," *The Tucson Citizen*, Tuesday, April 21, 1987.

Chapter 10 Taming the Alligator, Draining the Swamp

1. Forward and Torres, *Men Who Hate Women*, p. 287.

Chapter 11 How to Use "Choice Power" to Become a Positive Pleaser

1. Adapted from David Viscott, M.D., *Risking* (New York: Pocket Books, a Division of Simon & Schuster, Inc., 1983), pp. 72–75.

2. Viscott, *Risking*, pp. 135–36.

3. Judith Viorst, *Necessary Losses* (New York: Ballantine Books, 1986), p. 220.

4. Robert Karen, "Giving and Getting in Love and Marriage," *Cosmopolitan*, March 1987, p. 229.

5. Harley, *His Needs, Her Needs*, chapter 12.

6. All of the material on giving and getting was adapted from Robert Karen, "Giving and Getting in Love and Marriage," *Cosmopolitan*, March 1987, pp. 229–237.

7. Forward and Torres, *Men Who Hate Women*, p. 287.

Chapter 12 How to Please Yourself without Feeling Guilty

1. Baer, *How to Be an Assertive (Not Aggressive) Woman*, pp. 58–59.

2. Ibid., p. 99.

3. Ibid., pp. 20–23. See also the excellent chapters "Spotting Your Own Assertive Blocks," and "Exercise Class."

4. Edward R. Dayton and Ted W. Engstrom, *Strategy for Living* (Ventura, California: Regal Books, 1976), p. 65.

5. Ib id., pp. 67–69.

6. See Psalm 139 NIV.

Founder of MatchWise.com, internationally known Christian psychologist, award-winning author, radio and television personality, and speaker, **Dr. Kevin Leman** has ministered to and entertained audiences worldwide with his wit and commonsense psychology.

Best-selling author Dr. Leman has made house calls for *Focus on the Family* with Dr. James Dobson as well as numerous radio and television programs, including *Oprah*, *American Morning*, CBS's *The Early Show*, *Today*, and *The View*. Dr. Leman has served as a consulting family psychologist to *Good Morning America*.

Dr. Leman is the founder and president of Couples of Promise, an organization designed and committed to helping couples remain happily married. His professional affiliations include the American Psychological Association, the American Federation of Radio and Television Artists, the National Register of Health Services Providers in Psychology, and the North American Society of Adlerian Psychology.

Dr. Leman attended North Park College. He received his bachelor's degree in psychology from the University of Arizona, where he later earned his master's and doctorate degrees. Originally from Williamsville, New York, he and his wife, Sande, live in Tucson, Arizona. They have five children and one grandchild.

Discover how to make **birth order** work for you

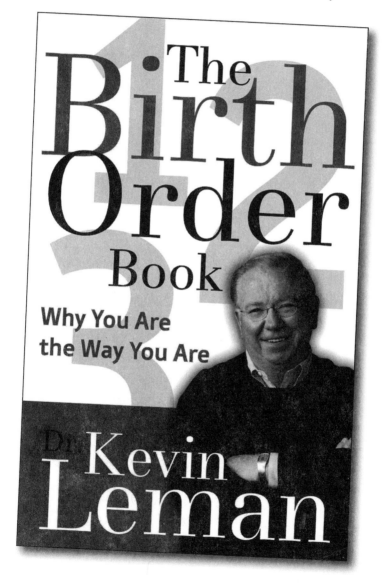

The Birth Order Book

Why You Are the Way You Are

Dr. Kevin Leman

Create a **Lifestyle** of
Passion *and* **Intimacy**

Creating Intimacy
to Make Your
Marriage Sizzle

Sex Begins
in the Kitchen

Dr. Kevin Leman

AUTHOR OF **THE BIRTH ORDER BOOK**

KID-tested, Parent-APPROVED

over **1 million** copies in print

Making Children MIND without Losing YOURS

Dr. Kevin Leman

Best-selling author of *The Birth Order Book*

A book for every

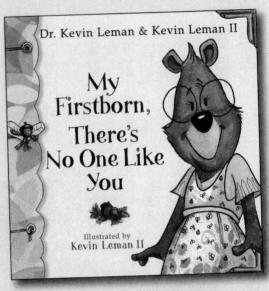

Dr. Kevin Leman & Kevin Leman II

My Firstborn, There's No One Like You

Illustrated by
Kevin Leman II

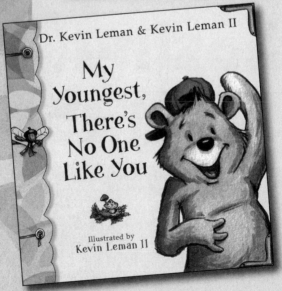

Dr. Kevin Leman & Kevin Leman II

My Youngest, There's No One Like You

Illustrated by
Kevin Leman II

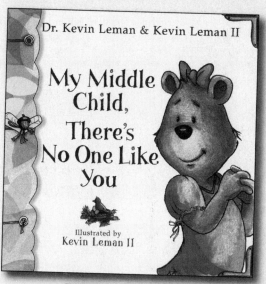
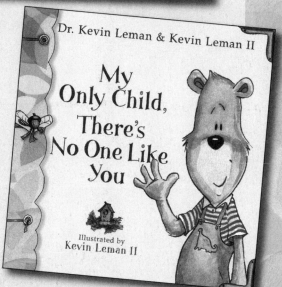